From
Goo To Gratitude

A Story of Healing from (and Thriving after) Narcissistic Abuse

KATHLEEN JOAN

ISBN: 979-8-9868905-0-0

Cover Design by Alyssa Noelle Coelho
Interior Design by Teagarden Designs

*This is dedicated to all those who constantly open their hearts,
rekindle their spirits, and seek better ways to love others well.*

Acknowledgments

"If there is light in the soul,
There will be beauty in the person.
If there is beauty in the person,
There will be harmony in the house.
If there is harmony in the house,
There will be order in the nation.
If there is order in the nation,
There will be peace in the world."

~ Chinese Proverb ~

To My Family and Friends

This book took almost three years from beginning to end. It was a labor of love and what support and encouragement has done for me. In the writing of it, I have come to realize all the people who have made it a reality. Heartfelt thanks to all my family and friends whose love and support over the years has been the foundation of this book. Many of you had no clue I was writing one but each of you have taught me so much and your contribution in my life has been so instrumental in the writing process.

I also want to thank Amanda Johnson and her team at True to Intention for helping me achieve my message goal. Without her suggestions, I couldn't possibly have shared my story with such clarity and vulnerability. She believed, like me, in the need for this knowledge to get out there and offered more than what she bargained for to help me finish. Thank you, my friend!

Contents

Introduction

"Our task is not to seek for love but to seek and find the barriers that we build against it."

~ Rumi ~

Heart racing, I jumped out of bed to shake it off. As I walked around the room, trying to catch my breath, I wondered silently to myself, *I never wake up feeling panicked. What could this be about?*

Almost as soon as I asked the question, an idea popped into my head and shocked me: *I need to check his cell phone.* As I tiptoed into the bathroom to retrieve it, I chastised myself, *I have no idea why I'm doing this. Invading someone's privacy really makes me nervous.*

But still, almost as if led by another power than my own, I unplugged his phone from the outlet, tiptoed out of the bedroom and into the living room, slipped into my favorite chair, and found hundreds of texts and emails between my husband and a woman I had befriended and welcomed into our home. I clasped my hand over my mouth, afraid to make a noise and wake him before I had the chance to see everything. My hands were shaking, and my heart pounded harder with every new text and email.

A few hours ago, I went to bed thinking all was well—that I was safe in the arms of someone I knew well. Our marriage was fine, and I had no reason to doubt the integrity of our relationship or his love for me. There has to be a good explanation. He couldn't possibly be lying straight to my face, keeping dark secrets, taking advantage of my trust. Surely, she's not taking advantage of my hospitality?!?

A few hours later, as I sat, heart still pounding, I wondered what in the world to do when he woke up later that morning.

Maybe I am just imagining all of this. It's impossible. They would never do that.

Waking Up is Hard to Do

Unfortunately, over the course of the next year, my best friend—the one I'd played with for over forty years—became a stranger as every explanation turned out to be false and every belief I thought to be true shattered and fell to the floor... laying there like pick-up sticks until I could figure out which "truths" to pick up again. The year was full of confrontations, apologies, attempts to heal our marriage, and more wake-up calls. For quite a bit of the journey, I didn't know what to think or say or do to move forward. I couldn't eat or sleep and didn't want to leave the house.

Prior to that wake-up call, I considered life to be pretty good. We had a nice home, a sailboat at the lake, two nice cars, and a motorcycle. Our three children were smart, beautiful, and healthy, with wonderful families and careers of their own. We had a supportive extended family, great friends who were lots of fun. During the week, we exercised, ate dinners, took walks, and watched TV together every evening. On weekends, we sailed, rode bicycles, attended plays, watched football games, and shared an array of other fun activities. After raising the kids, fighting the battles, and conquering life's challenges, we were empty-nesters, planning adventures we could never afford earlier in our life.

Externally, everything looked fine. There were no clues that anything wasn't what it appeared to be. I thought we had nailed marriage.

I was wrong, and it took years for me to get to the bottom of how wrong I was.

Answers for the Healing Journey

When it ended, people kept telling me to "let it go" and move on, making comments such as, "You never know what goes on behind closed doors." But I was behind those closed doors, and I had no clue what was going on. I needed to know what happened and began a quest to do all I possibly could do to find answers.

It was normal for me to find answers in Scripture. We were Christians since childhood, attended church faithfully, even led studies in our home. This time, Scripture didn't bring peace.

So, I went back to my biology roots. As I began studying, I discovered science has exploded since I had attended college four decades earlier. There's way more understanding now as to how the mind-body works. It started a domino effect that led to my ultimate liberation from a multitude of beliefs that had held me hostage my entire life—an awakening for me that I am determined to pass on to anyone who finds themselves in a similar situation.

What I found in my research helped me to understand how personalities are developed and the habitual beliefs that were driving my choices, compromising relationships, and damaging my health. When I learned about the Narcissistic/Codependent dynamic, my whole world suddenly made sense.

It wasn't easy to face all of this, and I was grateful that the science actually gave me additional pathways to transform beliefs at deeper levels than I would have been able to do without it. Coupled with good counsel, the support of family and friends, and many tips I found along the way, the science helped me heal and rebuild my life.

From Goo to Gratitude

Through all this study and personal work, I've come to realize that there's an art and a science to life and especially to the healing process for those of us recovering from Narcissistic/Codependent relationships. The art is the dream; the science is how to get there.

In the middle of my mess, I was manning the Butterfly Booth at the State Fair. As a Master Gardener, explaining the six-week cycle of a butterfly had been one of my volunteer "service acts" for several years. But this was the first year I associated my-self as being in the middle of something transformative—the upside-down phase. During transformation, the caterpillar forms a protective chrysalis that hangs upside-down. It's already consumed tons of leaves during the first few weeks and grown big enough to shed its outer skin multiple times before it formed its protective shell. When it enters the dark space of the chrysalis, its body literally dissolves into a liquidy, gooey mess. Nothing about the former self stays intact.

I felt like I was in that stage. This was the darkest time of my life as every single belief was questioned and every "rock-solid truth" disintegrated and dissolved into one big mess. I couldn't see my way out. I didn't want anyone to see me in the dark either. Hardly anyone knew what I was going through. Many admired our Christian family, and I was humiliated, embarrassed, and afraid to speak out. What I really wanted everyone to know was what I cried into my pillow in the dark hours of the night: *Why would he do this? I thought we were on the same page. We put God first, worshiped together, prayed together. I worked really hard to be there for him, did everything he wanted, practiced every single rule. God should be blessing us! What the heck? What is she doing that I'm not? I was so nice to her too. How dare her! This is so unfair!*

I was in the dark night of my soul, feeling angry, confused, ashamed, and guilty with no clue why I was there, what I had done wrong, or how to fix things.

The only thing I did know was what happened to the caterpillar after the chrysalis stage. Its disintegrated body would transform into a new creature, poke a hole through its protective shell, squeeze itself out, sit in the sun and dry off its new wings, look at its structure and colors, and know instinctively what to do next. It would leap, take off, and experience more freedom than it ever dreamed possible while it had been stuck on the stick eating leaf after leaf. That awareness inspired me to repeat my volunteer service every night that week. I needed the distraction, but I also needed the reminder that if I could just be patient, hang on just a little bit longer—long enough to get some answers—there would be light at the end of the tunnel.

As I became my own science experiment, I did get answers; but the outcome wasn't what I had hoped. My marriage dissolved. I began to observe, trust, and transmute emotions, and was led down a path that transitioned me from grief to a place of peace and understanding that's hard to describe. My body relaxed, more than it had in a long time. I had more compassion, less self-doubt, and much less confusion. In other words, I became a better version of me. All I can say now is a quiet and humble "thank you" as I go about my daily activities and especially as I spend time with my grandchildren and try to pass along these lessons while they are young.

In fact, a few weeks ago, I had one such opportunity. I was swimming with three of my grandkids in their backyard pool when suddenly everything went crazy. It started when my seven-year-old granddaughter freaked out over a small dead lizard in the water. She was pushing it away and screaming while her brother, age four, had stopped swimming and now clung to the side of the pool, clearly pondering what was going on. My youngest grandson, at one year of age, floated leisurely next to me with his floaties. Deciding that all was well with the boys, I rushed over to help my granddaughter. Meanwhile, their new puppy had heard her screams for help, rushed over and instinctively jumped in to "save" her. His splash caused a big enough ripple to topple the youngest over, even with his floaties. Hurriedly, I found and removed the lizard, calmed my granddaughter, got the dog out, and rushed back to the one with floaties to make sure he wasn't drowning. By the time I got to him, he had already turned himself right-side up and was wiping water away from his eyes. Wondering how traumatized he was, I asked if he was okay. A slight smile crossed his lips as he looked at me with his big, watery, loving eyes as if trying to understand the words he had just heard. And then with a one-year-old's curious, sweet, innocent, sincere voice, he said, "What the heck?" I heard those three words and my own eyes got watery. My mind flashed back to the many times I had used those words myself—at least a thousand times over the past several years—wondering "what the heck" was going on when my life was turned upside-down so quickly that morning years ago.

As I looked at my grandson's sweet face, I gulped back tears of gratitude. Because of that upside-down, I had the opportunity to trust—beyond any doubt—that everything is happening for me, not to me. I want to make sure that my grandchildren learn how to trust too, without falling prey to the limiting beliefs that had made my life so challenging.

I smiled back at him, wiped away the rest of the water from his eyes, gave him a big hug, and said, "Yep, Sweetie, you got it right. 'What the heck?' Those are exactly the words you can use for these kinds of moments. Great job!"

He didn't need to know it wouldn't be the last time he'd use them. But I did want him to know, in his first tender year of life, this feeling of upside-down is normal. These moments will happen throughout his life, and his ability to relax into the natural processes of life will develop depth of character. As he learns to handle life challenges and confusing moments that occasionally pop up, he can approach them with the same childlike curiosity, confident that no matter "what the heck" is happening, he has all the resources he needs to not be stuck upside-down for long. With a little bit of guidance from his grandma, he'll learn to use fearful experiences as feedback, develop the courage to move on, and gain resilience as he grows in stature and wisdom. His understanding of words and childhood associations that shaped his life will help him better grasp the core of who he is: love.

As I held him close, I felt gratitude for every upside-down I ever experienced. They all contributed to who I am now. With non-stop questioning and a lot of seeking and knocking on doors that were repeatedly slammed shut in my face, I became a different person—a more willing and able woman who can feel more, dare more, risk more, and trust more, despite the chaos happening around me. There's a new level of freedom I never knew existed—a new way of doing life that is much more easy, fun, and exciting.

Prevention and Intervention

I've heard it said messes become messages and pain becomes purpose. I'm out of the dark goo and more aware of how we all got into the messes we're in now. I'm ready to float on the winds that blow, waving my colorful wings—be a sign of hope for those who are trying to heal from toxic relationships and/or rebuild their lives and model for future generations as to what is possible when we surrender to the transformation process. They, too, can avoid a lot of unnecessary pain with the right knowledge and life skills.

What to Expect and Disclaimers

On the pages of this book, you will witness my own personal journey of transformation. I have struggled with how much of my story (and others' stories) to share, but I've been made to realize that this story is not just mine. It's the story of so many others who have grown up in a culture that has misunderstood ancient wisdom and is too far behind real science. It's the story of our collective grief as we look at the ways the Narcissist/Codependent dynamic has been so deeply embedded in our cultural systems. Though I have wanted to quit writing many times, I'm again pulled by another power than my own.

I can see the tapestry of my life tied together with the threads of all my experiences. It seems that my entire life has been in preparation for *such a time as this*. That phrase is from the Biblical character Esther. She wanted to tell the King her kingdom was in danger; but at the time, to approach the King would be breaking the rules and she could have been killed. In the end, she did it anyway, and her kingdom was saved. I know the feeling. It's always been safer to stay under the radar. I have tried writing this book with just scientific facts, not wanting to be vulnerable with my story. However, I wouldn't want to read a book on this topic without knowing the author had successfully overcome the same situation I was in. For a long time, I didn't think I could share my story like this. But there's a narcissism/codependency pandemic destroying our land and science came along just in time to save it. It worked for me. I'm a changed person and am compassionately committed to share my knowledge with others. I want to help restore lives back to emotional peace and harmony so that life can be enjoyed while here on Earth.

This book is an offering of the ancient wisdom and modern science I've discovered to help you understand why we do the things we do and create a new mindset for success. It will be invaluable and can be used the rest of your life—applied to any challenging situation, circumstance, or condition encountered.

What to Do When It's Hard to Read

There will be times when the content of this book will upset you. The stories might reveal some of your own thoughts, feelings, emotions, or circumstances. You might find yourself feeling confused, angry, sad, or a myriad of other emotions. When this happens, I recommend that you take a few deep breaths and relax, knowing that your body is working for you, not against you. Emotions carry a wealth of information and with an open mind and heart, we can understand their language. But know this: No matter what you're feeling, you're *not* broken. You may even need to take a break, and take time to let the words sink in, especially that last comment that *you are not broken.*

The Invitation

There's a Physics term called the "tipping point" that we've seen many times in history. It's that magical moment when an idea, trend, or social behavior crosses a threshold, tips, and spreads like wildfire. As we trust our hearts and transform our minds, my hope is that with time, education, and more aware-ness, we can turn the world upside-down and be a champion of all that's good.

CHAPTER ONE

Is this Your Cocoon or Mine?

Preventing, Fixing, and Saving

"Until you realize how easily it is for your mind to be manipulated, you remain the puppet of someone else's game."

~ Evita Ochel ~

As I sat going through my husband's phone that fateful morning, my mind flashed back to two conversations I'd had a few weeks earlier.

I had traveled to California to attend the gender reveal party planned for my son's second child and then to a conference in D.C., where my daughter was presenting some of her work. My husband had agreed that it was a good idea and even helped me find airline tickets for the three-legged flight—an unusual but appreciated gesture.

At the end of my stay with my son, I was sitting across from my daughter-in-law, waiting for him to take me to the airport for the second leg of my trip, when I remembered a conversation with a gal at the party. She had raved about how wonderful and helpful my son was as her youth pastor. When I shared her rave reviews with my daughter-in-law to tout the fact that her husband was one awesome guy, she responded abruptly with, "Who was she?"

The snippy comment, along with my look of surprise, inspired her to quickly add that the head pastor had asked her to be on guard for "eager eyes"—girls looking for male authority figures to fill the void of not receiving love from their own dad at home. He knew several leaders who had succumbed to "eager eyes" and was super cautious with himself and his staff. Practicing what he preached, he would never have conversation with a woman if they were the only two in the room and encouraged my daughter-in-law to be a watchful scout on her husband's behalf.

Wow, super-cautious, I had thought to myself and then shared how my husband had been told to do the exact opposite at his job. When I explained that he had been encouraged to mentor a female student, my son interjected, "Highly inappropriate, Mom," as he walked into the kitchen.

Highly inappropriate? Really? It had never occurred to me that his mentoring could be deemed inappropriate. In my husband's defense, I told them that he had even asked if I had any problems with him helping her prepare a resume during private lunches, cheer her on at sporting events, and include her at church and family dinners.

"I hadn't minded at all," I had told them, "I thought it was a really nice thing to do."

A short conversation followed about what was appropriate and inappropriate, and then we drove off to the airport.

A few hours later, I was having a glass of wine in D.C. with my daughter before heading up to our room. Enjoying our time with each other, catching up, taking in the fresh flowers in the atrium, I told her about the trip and the excitement at the party when a "boy" was announced with blue balloons. Then I shared some of the "eager eyes" conversation. Before I could ask her opinion, she choked on her wine and nearly came out of her chair. She said she'd been suspicious for months about her dad's mentoring role and viewed it as highly, highly inappropriate.

Wow! I thought "highly inappropriate" was bad, but highly, highly inappropriate?!? Oh No!

Concerned and wanting to warn my husband of this possible danger, I immediately called him. I was so concerned, not wanting him to lose his impeccable integrity among family and peers after so much personal career success. When I was unable to reach him that night, I couldn't sleep. My mind flooded with memories of moments of her laughing with him at football games, teasing with him at church, taking motorcycle rides with him, and even looking at him with sideway smiles at the dinner table while enjoying my home-cooked meals. I loved that she felt welcomed in our home and had never once suspected danger.

I wanted so badly to protect him that I slipped out of the conference the next day to call again. This time, he answered. Glad to hear his voice, I quickly asked how his week was going and then got to the real reason for calling. I tried to sound reasonable and non-accusatory, as I didn't want to make a big deal over nothing. He listened without interrupting and calmed my fears by saying he was more than willing to talk to her and step away from being her mentor in order to protect her from getting overly attached. It was such a relief, not only that he valued my love for him, but that he was so willing to do something about my fear. I hung up feeling reassured, went back to the conference, and enjoyed the rest of the time spent with my daughter in D.C. It was cherry blossom season with perfect weather—my idea of a fun mother-daughter weekend.

When I had returned home a few days later, I was greeted with two pots of spring flowers, warm hugs, and words that made me feel greatly missed. *Ahhh, it's always good to be home again!*

As we sat on the back patio, I shared stories and pictures, drank iced tea that he prepared, and thought, *Wow, maybe I should be gone more often. Flowers and tea? The house is clean, vacuumed, no dishes in the sink ...nice.*

After a while, I casually asked if he'd had the conversation and how she had handled it. He assured me that he had and that she had understood and handled it fine. *He always knows how to use words that sound so kind and tactful,* I smiled to myself, thankful that he had handled things so quickly and efficiently.

The very next day, I received a lengthy three-page letter via email. Contrary to his reassurance, she had not taken the conversation well at all. The letter indicated she was super angry and hurt that I mistrusted her, making comments like, "How dare you accuse me!"

I felt awful. To clear things up, I'd met with her for coffee, apologized, talked about the conversation I had with my son, explained my motives, and assured her that she wasn't being accused of anything—that my intention was to protect her and keep our relationship safe long-term. I could tell she was defensive, but the conversation seemed to end well. As we parted ways, I was just thankful we would be gone most of the summer and could put an end to all of this nonsense.

It was just a few weeks later that I found myself sitting on the sofa in the middle of the night going through my husband's texts and emails. When he woke up hours later and saw me with his phone, I threw it at him and asked him to explain. He blinked a few times and then calmly explained that my concerns in D.C. were valid—that he had already known she was getting overly attached when I called. He had been so understanding and agreeable on the phone because he had already confronted her and handled it. I was so surprised and disappointed that he hadn't confided in me, but more concerned for him that he had to deal with her unwanted advances all alone. He thanked me and expressed concern back, assuring me that danger was nipped in the bud and that he didn't say anything because he didn't want me to be concerned. His warm hugs, gentle touch, and soft, calming words enabled me to breathe a deep sigh of relief, embrace him back, and ask him what he wanted for breakfast. I went to the kitchen to prepare it and as we ate, the conversation switched to summer plans. We had a fun, full itinerary ahead.

We had a lovely summer and when classes were about to begin for the fall semester, the idea that she could lock eyes on him again soon prompted me to purchase a dozen cards and find a special place to put one each day. I wanted him to feel loved and never be tempted. One morning, as I searched for a new place to put a card, I saw a briefcase on the floor and wondered if he was using it. When I peeked inside, the only thing I found was a manila folder. I opened it to see if it had a date to indicate current use. What I found stunned me. It was a graphic, detailed love letter from her.

Suddenly, there was zero doubt that everything I had been told since before my trip, by both of them, was a bold-faced lie. After being so concerned for both of their welfare, I felt totally betrayed, angry, and ashamed that I had trusted anything they had said, much less every single word.

I was supposed to be getting ready for a brunch, my wet hair in a towel, but I couldn't breathe. My body shaking uncontrollably, I couldn't move. By the time he returned from golfing, I was reeling. I told him to get his things and get out. He refused to leave, insisting he wanted to work things out and would stay in the guest room until I got over my anger. There was no way he could deny the affair; but he told me they both realized how stupid it was, and there was no future in it. He was so, so sorry, apologized profusely, and asked if I could ever, forgive him. Notified of my discovery, she also came over to apologize and beg forgiveness through big tears.

When they both apologized and made sincere promises, I found myself wanting to believe, and thinking I should. *After all, it's the good and Christian thing to do, right?* But I was furious. *How could the two people I care for deeply and trust wholeheartedly just carelessly destroy what I view as something so special and sacred?* And I was even angrier with myself. *How could I have been so stupid... and so naïve? Why couldn't I see this?*

The Science of Being Blind to Reality

I was so confused as to how I could possibly have been so blind to so much of my husband's deception until I began to study the science of how our mind-body is formed from the time we are young.

Born innocent and precious, children come into the world with heart and mind wide open, ready to learn, curious, and with no agenda other than to explore the world and everything in it. We soak in every experience like a sponge, feel comfortable in our own skin, and perceive the world as magical and wonderful. Wired to connect, we trust our bigger-than-life caretakers and rely on them to take good care of us. We want to communicate our thoughts and desires, laugh when we are comfortable, and cry when in distress. We use our imaginations to play and daydream about life's possibilities.

But all of this gets educated out of us through experience.

When experiencing C.R.A.P. (criticism, rejection, abandonment, punishment), the fear of falling from favor in the eyes of someone we need and love can easily cause us to judge ourselves with thoughts of being bad, unworthy, or unlovable. Many of us have actually been told those things—not only once, but repeatedly—from a culture that didn't know any better.

Thoughts of being unworthy and rejected by those we love is extremely traumatizing to a child. It creates an incredible pressure to do things *right*. Each "failure" fans the flames of guilt and shame. Our bodies tense, muscles stiffen, the throat closes, the breath becomes shallow and our mind races to fix things. The fear of being *wrong* can forever haunt us with self-criticism, self-rejection, self-abandonment, and self-condemnation. The longer the trauma and fear stay unexpressed in the dark, the bigger they get.

Law of Association

Viktor Frankl, the neurologist, psychiatrist, and holocaust survivor who wrote *Man's Search for Meaning,* said, "Nothing has meaning until we give it a meaning." Two people in the same family can be in the same room and experience the same event yet one be fine and the other highly reactive. Once meaning is attached, the memory becomes part of our nervous system, stored for future reference.

Memory was designed for our good. It's the basis of immunity. The body recognizes a foreign invader, such as Covid, and tells the brain to form antibodies that will remember how to destroy it the next time it sees it. Any danger is remembered the same way. We were born with only two fears—the fear of loud noises and the fear of falling. Every other danger is learned and stored for future reference. This is how we learn to avoid running into streets, burning ourselves on hot stoves, and repeating the same mistakes over and over.

The body remembers everything. Neurons are developed the same way photographs used to be developed in the lab—unseen images are developed with chemicals in a dark room. Similarly, images in our imagination form neurons when we didn't understand words or know any better. The brain thinks in picture images, and every memory—good or bad, right or wrong—is stored in the body as a neuron, understood to be downloaded like an app in our nervous system. As neuroscientist Dr. Joe Dispenza explains it: "*What gets fired, gets wired.*" Our *perception* of pain or pleasure becomes our reality. By the age of seven, neurological wires run throughout our body.

The problem is that it is estimated that at least 75% percent of childhood was misinterpreted. True or not, if an event was perceived as "bad", the neuron will fire again and again when something similar shows up, even though the danger is long gone. The only person who can feel these neurons is you. And the only person who can do something about them is you.

The fear of being unworthy makes safety and security uncertain. It can happen as a result of a mistake or accident, or gross abuse or negligence. However it started, at some level, we all learned a response to the fear of being unworthy and rejected by those we love. We learned there was a right and wrong way to think, speak, and behave. To survive, we followed the rules, went with the flow, and continually adjusted to the feedback.

> "Mother is the name for God in the lips
> and heart of little children."
>
> ~ William Thackeray ~

Where It Started for Me

As the fourth child in a family of six kids, I had a front row seat to the impact of generational distress. Already emotionally fragile because of being raised in a home with an alcoholic dad, my mother had a "nervous breakdown" after doctors told her that her last child was born with Down's Syndrome. She was alone in the hospital room and decided to keep the news to herself so as not to ruin Christmas, or my sister's birthday in January, or another sister's birthday in February, or Easter in

March. Her silence continued until my dad noticed this child wasn't developing like the others had.

After he discovered the diagnosis and how much help my brother would need and sought the advice from the pediatrician and the church, he decided to place my new brother in a state home. My mom was devastated. It tipped her fragile emotional state over the edge, probably triggering her own memory of being rejected and abandoned as a child. The "tip" didn't happen suddenly overnight but unraveled slowly as the result of her lifelong pattern of not knowing how to handle common emotions in a healthy way. Her father had numbed his with alcohol, and my mom tried to survive hers by hiding sadness and sorrow. Repressing grief is like trying to hold beach balls underwater. Balls are naturally buoyant, and that effort takes a constant toll. Neurological ruts deepened over the years and my mom's mental health worsened. My dad tried to get her help several times, but the only thing physicians knew to do at the time was prescribe medication. She hated how they made her feel and eventually stopped. Unresolved, toxic emotions swirled, creating deeper and deeper neurological ruts. Pain took over her life. Convinced that no one understood and that everyone was against her, she decided to file for divorce and left the family.

When she left, I was thirteen. Because I saw how much my mom suffered with unwarranted suspicion and hostility, I decided to make our family safe and prevent additional pain. *I won't worry them. I won't complain. I won't ask for too much. I'll keep the peace. I'll smile and be okay.*

The way I survived was to stay under the radar. I didn't want to make any more trouble than what was already swirling in our home; so, I decided to be good, get straight A's in school, and never complain or ask for anything. I was more concerned for my dad, my mom, my brother, and other siblings. I wanted them to be okay, so I tried to be okay.

It's easy to see how I carried this same childhood pattern into adulthood and my marriage—how I learned to turn a blind eye to my own emotions and be more concerned for the welfare of others. Not only had my mother modeled this, but the verbiage in my religious training also confirmed that "denying self and serving others" was, in fact, the good Christian thing to do.

In my mind, I was doing the right and Godly thing by remaining silent, sweeping sadness under the rug, and paying attention to everyone else's emotions and needs but my own. I didn't want to be a problem, and I wanted my family to appear "normal." In fact, my niece often joked that we seemed like the "Leave it to Beaver" family.

> "Be careful how you think; your life is
> shaped by your thoughts."
>
> ~ Proverbs 4:23 ~

Science 101: How the Brain Works—
The Amazing Human Intellect

Thoughts create things. We all know this at some level. For example, the chair I'm sitting in was a thought in someone's mind before it became a chair. Someone had to think about it before it became a thing. The clothes I'm wearing began with a thought. Someone had to think about the design before giving it to a seamstress. Things don't "just happen," but most of us don't understand the true power of really knowing that everything begins with a thought.

Our mind listens to what we say and, and its one purpose is to keep us safe. So, if I say to myself, "I'm a loser. I'll never get a break in life," my brain believes it. Its job is to respond. Keep me safe. And it does so, with thousands of chemical reactions per second. It automatically matches the picture, and makes cortisol—a stress hormone—that will make me *feel* as if I'm a loser and will never get a break in life.

Words have power. Thoughts are invisible words that become physical form.

In other words, our inner thought world creates how we feel about our outer world.

The mind, body, and spirit can't be divided or parceled out as if they're separate entities. If one is negatively affected, the others are affected. A fearful image in our mind can put knots in our stomach and affect how the body feels. Any physical, emotional, or spiritual aspect out of balance pushes the others out of balance. We will see visible results in health, goals, and motivation.

Unfortunately, the specialists in these three fields don't really talk to each other. You'd think they'd be getting together every year in conferences, or something, but that's not the case. The mind specialists have their own psych lingo; the body specialists have medical lingo for every single bone, joint, and organ; and the spiritual gurus have lingo for every religion out there. We've basically been in what I call a game of "referral ping-pong" to understand why our lives aren't working smoothly—the way they were intended. But few are seeing us as a complete, whole, functional unit—the way we are designed.

In other words, we have two languages to learn—an external language and an internal language.

> "Thoughts are the language of the mind.
> Emotions are the language of the body."
>
> ~ Dr. Joe Dispenza ~

Humans are a field of conscious and subconscious thoughts. Similar to a computer, the conscious (what we're focused on) would be what we can see on the computer screen; while the subconscious (what's felt in the body) would be thoughts in the mainframe running the system. While we have access to unlimited information with the internet, when emotions are off limits, myopic minds often think the little bit of data seen on the screen in front of them is all there is to know.

Thoughts are necessary to survive *and* to thrive. Thoughts are how we connect and protect ourselves, how we plan our goals, and how we learn to stay safe. We don't have to believe them all. Emotions become our truthteller. They carry a wealth of information; and they're here to help guide us, correct us, encourage us, and help us to be courageous to take the next step forward. Since they were always considered taboo, I did what I could to avoid them, let them go, push them away, bright-side them, or find the silver linings.

It's important to note that emotions are not the same thing as "being emotional." Emotions are the subtle cues that show up automatically, such as blushing when embarrassed, hands shaking when nervous, a gut flip when wary, or the "ahh" factor when safe at home. According to grief counselor David Kessler, each emotion *means* something, which isn't the same thing as understanding. For example, there is no meaning in a murder, a child drowning or someone dying of cancer. It's impossible to understand that kind of loss. Loss is not a test, a lesson, something to handle, a gift, or a blessing. Loss is what happens in life. Meaning is what we make happen *after* loss.

Emotions are what make us human. And listening to the body is critical to listening to Divine inspiration. We need "spiritual" eyes to notice the spirit with which we do things. And science backs up the fact that transformation doesn't "just happen" with cognitive analysis alone. Intellect isn't enough. Emotions have to be included, noticed in the current moment, to transform and make good decisions.

But, sadly, most of us don't listen. Our culture deemed emotions irrelevant, and they became a foreign language. We learned not to trust them, made them small, and used willpower to control and dominate them. As a result, most of our time is spent in virtual reality, "lost in thought," feeling criticized, rejected, abandoned, or punished (CRAP!) without really knowing why.

Yet, when we compare the mind versus the body, there's a 5:95% percent mind to body ratio. This means 95% percent of our thoughts—the blueprint for making our choices—are hidden. And we're clueless—often doing what seems "right" but feels bad and doing what seems "wrong" but feels good.

This is exactly the reason I was blind to the affair that was happening right underneath my nose. I had been raised to do everything I could to ignore the body's natural cues. It became a tug-of-war between trusting my emotions versus trusting the words of another.

Despite feeling betrayed, hurt, and angry, I considered my marriage to be a worthy investment, and I wanted my life back. I believed it was still good and thought the affair was a wayward moment.

I chose to forgive them both, but I had no idea how to get past the anger or the anxiety I felt after losing trust.

We've always been good at handling crises in the past. Together, there has never been a problem too big to conquer.

Believing I needed to be more loving and attentive, I tried harder "to love well," which had been the intention I had set for the year when the pastor had challenged us to choose one. I had a thousand questions, but I didn't want to ask them or discuss the affair, thinking that it would be insensitive and add shame to his huge embarrassing mistake. Instead, I offered him compassion and understanding. But I was an emotional wreck.

This is way bigger than I ever imagined. Bigger than I know how to handle!

Not wanting to ruin his good reputation, I kept quiet and didn't say a word to anyone. I looked online for help on how to survive. When I found a Christian psychologist, a husband/wife ministry team that specialized in affairs, I emailed them and received a reply within fifteen minutes. They wanted me to participate on a national radio show in exchange for a free book, along with on-air tips for how marriages can survive affairs. I agreed and to protect his reputation, I used an alias.

I went into the interview convinced that I must be the problem, or not as good as *her*, and the one that needed tips on how to become more loving and appealing. These two psychologists confirmed what I already knew to be true by stating that I could make better choices and do more to meet his needs. I read their book when it arrived in the mail and used all their tips: I smiled more, made special dinners, planned romantic evenings, and even booked a trip to St. Maarten—a place I knew he always wanted to go. I tried everything I could think of to be more lovable and do all the right things. It appeared we had made it over the hump.

Wow! Those tips really did the trick!

My Upside-Down Invitation to Come Home to The Heart of Who I Am

Several months after the big confrontation and assurance from my husband, I had another panic attack from "out-of-the blue." This time, my first thought was to find the unused iPad in the attic. I knew it was still attached to his devices.

It didn't take but a day to discover that sincere promises were anything but the truth. This time, I decided against confrontation... at least until I knew more. The next several months could be pulled straight out of a riveting spy novel. I became an undercover investigator.

Each morning, I'd pull the iPad out from underneath the mattress to spy on texts and emails throughout the day and hide it before he came home in the evening. He'd walk out the door each morning, assuring me of his love and fidelity, only to tell her the same thing within minutes—even before leaving the driveway.

I tracked him throughout the day, greeted him warmly when he came home in the evening, and acted as if I knew nothing. The irony of all this was that he was the one who had spent twenty years in law enforcement as an undercover investigator. For me to be one was comical—and maddening. While serving dinner in the evening, I looked carefully at his body language when he answered my casual questions. False answers were given quickly and automatically, without batting an eye. There was absolutely no way I could tell he was lying—and I looked closely.

The saga continued a while longer. Not only did it take months to adjust to what I was seeing, but at this stage of my journey, I still believed, *If I just try harder, things will change.*

But they didn't.

It was time to get outside help.

CHAPTER TWO

Dissolving Foundations into Goo

Awakening and Researching

"One doesn't have to operate with great malice
to do great harm. The absence of empathy
and understanding are sufficient."

~ Charles M. Blow ~

When I'd finally had enough, I confronted him and asked him to leave. He tried to wriggle out of it again; but this time, his pleas and sincere-sounding words fell on deaf ears. He refused to leave, so I did.

"I'm not coming home until you get help!" I exclaimed tearfully and slammed the door shut on the way out. I had no idea where I was going. I just knew I needed to leave.

I finally broke the news to my sister. The next morning, while at her house, I received a text from him, explaining that he had contacted a pastor who knew us well and was willing to chat with us.

Yes! Thank goodness!

After hearing both sides of the story a few days later, the pastor advised us to get professional counseling. Fortunately, our church had professional help readily available; and I signed us up. We were given two counselors—one for me and one for "us." The pastor's wife offered to walk me into the office for my first appointment, and I was so grateful she wrapped her arm around my shoulder. My knees were wobbly. In addition to having to share my shameful story with someone, I was afraid of running into someone I knew.

It doesn't matter. I just need to figure out what needs to be fixed for our marriage to survive.

As soon as I sat down, I began to pour out the details of the previous five months to the kind lady in front of me, trying to be as accurate as I could possibly be so she could precisely diagnose my problem.

What in the world is she writing? I wondered to myself as she furiously took copious notes. *I'll distract her and glance over at the notebook.*

Because it seemed childish and I wasn't sure I was prepared to see what she was writing about me, I ignored the impulse and continued talking and answering questions during the short forty-five-minute session. When our time was up, I braced myself for her diagnosis, but she didn't give me one. She just thanked me for sharing and said she would see me after our couples counseling session. Disappointed that there was no diagnosis, I was still thankful she knew most of what had happened and that I wouldn't have to repeat it.

Several weeks later, couples counseling began. He and I met in the lobby and waited together. I felt hopeful, convinced this was what would get us back on track. When we were called into the office, I sensed he might be nervous, like me.

I reached over to touch his hand and said, "This is good. It'll be fine."

He whispered back, "Don't embarrass me in there."

Are you kidding me? I thought to myself as I pursed my lips to stay silent. *As if he hasn't already done that to himself?*

My intention was to get to the bottom of things by telling the truth, nothing but the truth. Embarrassment was nothing compared to the total humiliation and shame I felt.

After a short introduction to the process, the distinguished gentleman dove right in.

"Do you want to stay in the marriage?" he asked me first.

"Of course," I answered.

"And you?" he directed the question to my husband.

"Yes," my husband said while quietly nodding.

"Kathleen, how did his affair make you feel?" he asked gently.

Feel? What does that matter? Oh, I guess I could show him, I thought as I reached down to pull the picture out of my purse. Thankfully, I had attended a young mom group earlier that day as a mentor. The facilitator had asked the women to choose a picture from dozens of magazines to describe how they felt that day, and I had chosen one of a cold, lonely lake surrounded by a forest of trees that had been leveled to the ground. As I handed it to him, I said, "Everything I know to be true was leveled to the ground like these trees. I feel like I'm in the cold, still water of the lake—too numb to know what to think anymore."

He turned to look at my husband. "Tell me why she shouldn't kick you to the curb."

"I want to be the guy to get her out of the lake," he quickly replied and smiled at me.

Who knows if that's the truth? I thought as I forced a smile back.

"Is the affair over?" the counselor asked.

"Yes," my husband nodded.

"Would you like to respond?" he asked me.

"I know for a fact they met this morning," I said matter-of-factly, having seen on the iPad that morning that the two of them planned to meet while I was in my mom group.

He looked at my husband. "Is that true?"

My husband nodded but explained he met with her in person ...to let her down gently.

The counselor laughed and told my husband he was addicted to lying and needed to stop.

Why did he laugh? I wondered to myself. *Isn't it a good thing that he let her down gently and put a stop to this once and for all?*

At the end of the session, I felt encouraged until my husband said, "You embarrassed me in there. Who does he think he is to call me a liar? He doesn't know me. I don't like his accusations, and I don't think he's competent. I don't want to go back to this guy."

Seriously? I thought as I rolled my eyes without him seeing me. *He's been hired by the church. He's licensed. He's convenient. He seemed fine. How can you tell he's not competent after one session? But, then again, maybe we need someone we both like...*

"Let me think about it," I said quietly as we went our separate ways at the door.

During my next visit with my counselor, I asked whether I should find a different couple's counselor.

She slowly sank into her chair and gently but firmly said, "No. The one you have is fine. I consider him to be one of the top five psychologists in the city capable of dealing with this type of marriage."

"What do you mean, 'this type' of marriage?" I asked.

"Narcissistic/Codependent," she replied matter-of-factly.

"Which one am I?" I wondered out loud.

"You're the Codependent." She smiled kindly in my direction.

I'm codependent? No, I'm not! I'm independent! I mentally argued as self-righteous indignation reared up from within, especially since the nature of my husband's careers kept him away from home a lot, and I managed and handled nearly everything on my own. I wanted to challenge her diagnosis, but thought I better do some research before opening my mouth.

I was relieved at the same time.

Great! Now I know what to fix. The hard part is over. Let's get things back to normal!

I left her office, drove home, and immediately switched my online research from "affairs" to the two terms she had given me. Now that I had the conclusion, I just had to find the cause. I was good at fixing things.

Narcissism and Codependency

Narcissists are commonly understood to be people who look in the mirror at themselves and act proud, cocky, and arrogant. But the truth about narcissists is that there are covert types who appear charming, humble, and kind while, behind the scenes, they will use outright lies and oily manipulation to be in control and get what they want. When the Codependent becomes emotionally numb and stops reacting to pretty much anything the Narcissist says and does, the Narcissist will go on the prowl for someone new—someone easier to trigger (something commonly referred to as "narcissistic supply").

Codependents are commonly understood to be needy and clingy. But the truth about codependents is that most think it is selfish to be needy. They think they are an imposition, undeserving of someone's time and attention, and believe it is more virtuous to serve others than to be served. Most are self-reliant, worker-bees, and great at multitasking. The only problem is, they have to "depend" on feedback to know how well they're doing. (The term is actually being changed among psychologists to Self-love Deficit Disorder (SLDD).)

We all have some healthy Narcissistic/Codependent traits. To have a healthy sense of self and feel confident to hold high standards for how we want to be treated is a good thing. It is also important for us to remember that we share the planet and our lives with other people who do not share our ideas, and yet deserve the same respect.

These two personality types represent the masculine mind (direct, decisive, and driven) and the feminine heart (kind, compassionate, and considerate) within each one of us. When they work together, in tandem, we can be a healthy, balanced person. When they work independently, separately from each other, there can be some imbalance; and it can be destructive. But what is it that causes that imbalance?

The fear of being unworthy.

Both the Narcissist's and the Codependent's foundations are filled with beliefs which keep them ashamed of themselves, wondering whether they will ever measure up to someone's expectations.

Narcissist and Codependent personality types are on opposite sides of the same coin—the coin being our basic human need to be loved and respected by the community we live in. Narcissists lack empathy and learned to cope with emotions by projecting what they feel onto others to extract empathy. Codependents, on the other hand, have lots of empathy, but think it is for others and not themselves. They absorb what others feel, treat others the way they want to be treated—with compassion and understanding—but believe they are too unworthy to expect the same treatment in return. They justify poor behavior for the sake of the relationship and "lose themselves" while worrying about the concerns and needs of everyone around them.

Both consider their own emotions off limits and become like a human magnet, trying to control the other "so I can feel better."

Basically, both are looking for love in all the wrong places. Neither feel they can do enough, be enough, or say enough to be worthy; and both constantly question whether they're being loved and respected. Their brains have been hijacked and they search for someone or something "out there"—anywhere but inside their unworthy, unlovable selves—to fill the void. Relationships devolve into a toxic kind of love that's detrimental for all parties involved.

How We Got Here

The simple but uncomfortable truth is that we have grown up in a culture that devalued emotions and valued intellect. With an obedient heart and a ton of courage, many of us did what we were told. It became habit to comply and, "do" worthy things and rely on something "out there" to manage what we feel. The unexpected result was that we became emotionally unstable and ego-driven.

Narcissists created an over-inflated ego to cope with the fear of being unworthy and their inability to express it. They fear emotions, consider them weak and insecure, and reject being vulnerable—which means they have very little appreciation for, or understanding of, any emotion. They set up scenarios to play a savior role—someone strong and impermeable—to avoid being unworthy. They also become arrogant, think everyone with emotions is lesser-than, and aren't willing to take instruction from anyone they consider beneath them. When emotions make the Narcissist feel uncomfortable, they blame and shame with the idea that there is something the other isn't doing right. It can't be their actions, patronizing tone, or broken promises because *they* do everything right.

Codependents are at the opposite end of the spectrum. In response to the fear of being unworthy and the inability to express it, they developed an inferior ego and play the martyr role. They tend to be overly empathic, love to make others feel comfortable, and willingly give of themselves to make others feel good about themselves. When others are unhappy, they feel unhappy, are quick to sympathize, and jump through hoops to make things right. They martyr themselves on the altar of virtue just to win peace and almost get destroyed in the process as they allow others to "nail them to the cross"— thinking it's the *loving* thing to do.

Healthy people want to appreciate, nurture, be considerate and accommodate others, but Codependents go overboard. They take on guilt and shame that doesn't belong to them and blame themselves for not doing enough. As they try to make everyone be okay, they fix uncomfortable consequences that do not belong to them either. Rather than have the person experience normal painful consequences in order to learn how to deal with their own irresponsible choices, Codependents alleviate pain while undermining their own and take on a job that's not theirs to fix.

> "Until you make the unconscious conscious it
> will direct your life and you will call it fate."
>
> ~ Carl G. Jung ~

How I Got Here

As I explored the roots of my Codependency, I discovered that at some point, I had made the decision to be "nice" no matter how I was being treated. I placed a wooden plaque above the door that read, "As for me, and my house, I will serve the Lord," and I believed it was "the right thing to do"—the way to "love my neighbor" and be a good Christian.

The God of my upbringing was perceived "out there" somewhere and viewed all of humanity as separate, broken, and unworthy. My perception was that if I didn't "invite Him into my heart" and obey every single rule to a tee, things would go to hell in a handbasket—with me in it. To be a good Christian, I was taught to serve others first—consider myself *less-than*—as if we were all on a hierarchal totem pole of worth. As God is perfect, I wanted to be perfect and felt obligated to stifle, ignore, and tolerate my emotions as I tried to meet the expectations of God and everyone around me. When sad, disappointed, or frustrated, it seemed more loving to want what others wanted. I hesitated to speak up, minimized my disappointment, didn't want to be a burden, and stayed under the radar. I minimized my talents and interests as well, played small so others could play big. When my motives were misunderstood or told I wasn't doing a good enough job, I apologized and worked harder to do better. A veil of guilt hung over me whenever I was criticized for saying, doing, or being the wrong thing. But I was proud of myself for being a good Christian—someone "nice."

When I became a wife, my purpose was to honor God and make a difference in the lives of others. Even though childrearing was often tedious, I loved my family and wanted to inspire, nurture and raise healthy children. It brought joy and fulfillment to live my life with meaning, purpose, and significance. I hoped to connect emotionally with my husband and wanted him to feel loved and appreciated when he came home from work and can't remember a time when I didn't have dinner on the table, the house picked up, and the kids well-behaved—only to one day see clearly that he thought nothing about how I felt... or about anything at all. I was the one meeting with doctors, shopping, cooking, cleaning, organizing, doing the laundry, and managing finances while he went to work and pursued his career. But it was fine. I considered us a team, raising a family together. Subconsciously, I said yes to all his requests and worked my tail off, hoping he would be satisfied, as well as appreciate, respect, and love me back—actions I never learned to do for myself.

I realize now that my entire life was all about serving and taking care of everyone else, but for all the wrong reasons. I believed that if I were a good wife and mother, and took care of everyone else but myself, that I would be taken care of in return. When being a selfless martyr didn't bring the return I expected, I would get upset. Yet, whenever I discussed my frustration, the problem got turned around to be *my* problem. I was told, "We'll have to agree to disagree," or "That's ridiculous," or "You must be kidding." My feelings were totally ignored. Somewhere in my mind, I thought maybe we just had two different ways to express love. I figured if I did everything he wanted, he would eventually "see it" and want to reciprocate by doing something I wanted. Love could conquer all, right?

But that day never came. What (subconsciously) drove my behavior was the fear of losing my *image* of being a "good Christian wife."

Mario Martinez, a clinical neuropsychologist, says all groups wound their members with three tools: shame, abandonment, and betrayal. Shame is the fear of being selfish; abandonment is the fear of being alone; betrayal is the fear of having your group disrespect you. To quote Brené Brown: "Guilt says I made a mistake; shame says I *am* a mistake."

As I studied the science, I realized both of us had been living in survival mode for most of our lives. I saw how we both had shoved emotions beneath the surface to defend, fix, and save the other—all the while believing we needed to be defended, fixed, and saved.

Knowing that beliefs were indoctrinated at a young age, I began questioning every belief that taught me to fear and put me in defense mode. I wanted to "let go" of anything wreaking havoc on my ability to make good choices on my behalf from this point forward.

I discovered many beliefs that had been downloaded into my computer-brain and created a list for the top dozen. Instead of FEAR being interpreted as False Evidence Appearing Real, I entitled it...

False Entries Assumed Right

1. I am unworthy.

2. I am to believe God is with me, but I can't trust me.

3. I am broken—undeserving of love.

4. Jesus is God's one and only son. (Who am I?)

5. I am small and God is big.

6. Emotions are irrelevant.

7. I can do nothing; God is in control.

8. I am incapable of making good choices.

9. I am to "deny self and serve others" first.

10. I am to obey the rules, think, say, and do whatever authorities say.

11. I am meant to suffer through this life to enjoy the next one.

12. I am to "let go" offenses repeatedly.

These are just a few of the tenets at the core of my behavior when my husband dismissed my feelings over the course of our marriage.

When he went to play golf on our first Thanksgiving together, I was disappointed that he didn't want to enjoy the day together but didn't complain, stayed home alone... and made dinner to please.

When he left to play the day our first child was born, I minimized my overwhelm with the responsibility of being a new mom and justified his choice with the thought he probably felt overwhelmed with the responsibility of being a new dad.

When he "forgot" me at restaurants, or "forgot" his promise to pick me up at a certain time, I was irritated as I sat and waited anxiously, sometimes for hours; but I was the one who apologized when he was annoyed with my reaction.

When he "forgot" our agreement to handle chores together on a Saturday morning, I often did them alone just to get them done.

When he "forgot" to pick up an ingredient I needed for dinner—an agreement he made five minutes before he left work—I was surprised he could be so forgetful, but I shrugged it off or went to get it myself.

When he dismissed my request to stop moving my purse without telling me—leaving me to hunt all over the house for it—I simply hid it so he couldn't find it.

When he dismissed my desires to not move or start a business that I wasn't thrilled about starting, I rationalized it by saying, "It must be a good deal. I'll do what he wants."

Each incident could be considered minor on its own. However, over time, it became habit to do what he wanted and to not expect him to show up for anything important or count on him to follow through with anything he said he'd do. I simply found a solution. I either made excuses, defaulted to what he wanted, took over responsibilities, or simply adjusted. My goal was to put him, his needs, his goals, and his comfort above my own; and I shoved my needs, my goals, and my comfort to the background and lowered all my expectations to keep the peace, believing that this was "the right thing" to do. I had no idea that we were each playing our roles perfectly in this Narcissistic/Codependent relationship.

It was such a habitual pattern to ignore my feelings and consider others first that it took a while to even notice the emotional cues. I wouldn't have been able to notice without both counseling and science. Blind spots are labeled "blind" for good reason. Counseling sessions were filled with questions, and I became glued to the research.

Not only did I keep reverting back to the old pattern of trying this or that "one more thing" to help my husband make good choices on our behalf, but I invited my pastor over, well-versed in the original Hebrew meaning of words, to make sure that scripture and science were congruent. I spent hours and hours studying, taking words apart, and researching the new ideas and concepts. I couldn't stop. It almost felt like an obsession. But in the end, it was worth it. I understand now as to how our brains get wired with much more clarity regarding the habitual thoughts and patterns driving our Narcissist/Codependent culture.

As the weeks and months went by, more lies were uncovered; and it became obvious that my "one more thing" was my Codependent "fix-it" pattern. A ton of bricks instantly fell off my shoulders when my counselor assured me that I was *not* responsible for his behavior—that he had free will, just like me. However, my fear of losing the relationship and my "good Christian girl" image caused me to allow his irresponsible and callous choices to continue. Fear kept me blind to his attempts for control and unable to say, "No more!"

I could easily be kind and stand up for others when they were treated unkindly, but I couldn't stand up for myself. I was addicted to "denying self and serving others."

Subconscious fear was affecting other choices as well. I was often afraid to step out of my comfort zone out of fear I'd offend someone. I didn't like receiving compliments out of fear I'd be considered proud; I didn't want expensive items out of fear I'd be considered "uppity"; I didn't want to push my agenda out of fear I'd be considered selfish; I didn't want to try bigger things that would put myself "out there" out of fear I'd be criticized—like writing this book.

It also prevented me from seeing how God can coordinate things and bring everything back to balance without my help whatsoever.

Then one day, my brain suddenly shifted, and I clearly saw the world of manipulation I had been living in for decades.

I was still in counseling, but my husband had decided to switch from couples counseling to meeting with the pastor on sailing dates. I never questioned their conversations, but their talks seemed to be going well. I thought the affair was behind us, and the trip to St. Maarten with my daughter and her husband was a week away. Certain that everything was looking up, I went along my daily business, not realizing that my life was about to change forever.

It was a Sunday evening when I asked him a simple question, "What would you like to have to drink with dinner?" and received no response. Trying hard to be patient and loving, I was carefully watching my words and tone. To avoid becoming frustrated with his slow response, I looked down at my watch to time myself before repeating the question.

After waiting a full two minutes, I asked, "Did you hear me?"

No answer.

I set the timer again, waited, and repeated it a third time, a little more emphatically. "Did you hear my question?"

He jumped out of the chair and said that he had been thinking about it, that I should be slower to get upset, and that he refused to tolerate such disrespect. Stunned, I apologized over and over for my simple question being perceived as disrespectful. But he was so upset that he decided to stay in a motel that night—to take a breather from my "anger issues."

What the heck? I feel like I'm walking on eggshells already. No matter how hard I try, it keeps happening. How do I get him to answer one simple question? Maybe I should never ask a question? My stomach knotted and jaw clenched. *Maybe I should be a Stepford wife and walk around with a pasted smile on my face? Maybe I should just say "yes sir," "no sir," "three bags full, sir."*

Even after apologizing multiple times and pleading with him to stay, I watched him pack his things and walk out of the door. I was filled with guilt, frustration, and even hostility.

My eldest daughter called while I was still shaking my head in disbelief. A parallel experience at her workplace was causing her to deal with people falsely accusing her of motives she didn't have. Both of us were being emotionally pummeled, on a journey together, but wanting to learn how these people tick and how to respond in a Godly way.

When she heard what had happened, she was convinced he was still involved with the young woman. I doubted it and the passwords on his devices had recently been changed, so I couldn't "spy" on his phone. His emails seemed fine the past month, and he kept saying he was excited about our upcoming trip. She convinced me to go to the motel, where he said he was staying, to prove it. I thought it was ridiculous, but I did it just to prove to her that she was wrong.

Unfortunately, she was right. He wasn't there.

I didn't fall for it again, did I? I wondered as I drove around the parking lot a few times, wanting so badly for his car to be there somewhere. I checked every motel nearby just in case I heard the wrong name. After wandering and looking for hours, I finally drove home past midnight and tossed and turned all night, replaying events over and over in my head, feeling angry, hurt, confused, and made a fool all over again.

When my daughter texted early the next morning and learned he wasn't where he said he would be, she called and convinced me to fill my Yeti cup with coffee, go park near the woman's house, and wait to see if he was there.

This spying is getting more and more nerve-wracking, I thought as my stomach knotted.

She insisted, and I finally agreed. I drove to the house and parked my car nearby. She delayed going to work and stayed with me on the phone, drinking her coffee a thousand miles away, while we waited together.

While there, she suggested I text him to see if he had slept well and ask if he'd like to go to the gym at our normal time. I did. When he agreed, I snickered at the idea of me beating him at his own con game, especially since he had spent a career as one. But with trembling hands and heart pounding, I videotaped the garage door opening and saw his car.

But wait! The door closed. *What the heck?*

After waiting twenty more minutes and getting angrier, I texted again, "I know you're in there. You're the one who needs to go to work. I can wait here all day. No need to play hide-and-seek."

Twenty minutes later, I started the video again as he pulled out of the garage, pale as a ghost when caught red-handed. Then I pulled into the driveway, put the car in park, went to the front door, and angrily slammed my fists until she opened it. "I hoped you liked America. You're going back to your own country!" I yelled as she slammed the door in my face.

My daughter was on the next flight and in my living room four hours later.

As we sat there, my husband texted me to indicate that he wanted to meet and work things out—if I could get my "anger issues" under control.

She read the text and asked, "Is he always so manipulative?"

I had no idea what she was talking about.

"Mom, look at this…" she pointed. "This is so manipulative."

I simply couldn't see what she saw. Every time she talked about it, it was as if my brain saw the words from his perception of me, which correlated with mine—indicating *that I was the problem*. My daughter knew I had no "anger issues" and that he was blame-shifting. She was so angry that she would throw the phone on the couch, trying to get me to stop responding to his texts, explaining that I shouldn't be defending myself. "He is the one that should be making amends, on hands and knees, begging for forgiveness!"

But to be polite, I kept texting back, trying to clear up all the misunderstandings.

For the next few days, she pointed out the manipulation in line after line, with text after text. Suddenly, on the third day, my mind shifted to where I could see it.

I could almost feel cells morphing in my brain. I had been in counseling six months at this point and reading the research about how my brain was so entrained to think a certain way. So many beliefs were blocking me from seeing clearly. But in this moment, I SAW IT. Words that had been previously perceived through a cloudy lens suddenly became clear in their intention and meaning.

It was time. It was time to get out of the goo and get rid of the deeply-rooted neurological loops in my psyche that allowed this man to get away with manipulative behavior. It was not only cruel and mean-spirited, but it went against every one of my values that believed in morals such as truth and honesty... and treating people with dignity and respect.

The only way to reprogram my brain was to notice emotions. And unless he was willing to take 100% responsibility for his programming and find ways to regain my trust, I would guard my heart and stay away—no matter what he chose to do.

But where will I start?

CHAPTER THREE

Becoming a New Creature

Listening and Leaving Intact

"The real voyage of discovery consists not in
seeking new landscapes but in having new eyes."

~ Marcel Proust ~

Sitting at the kitchen table in the beach house, looking out at the beautiful landscape of St. Maarten, my heart was broken and heavy with disappointment that my husband and I wouldn't be playing together as I had imagined and intended for this trip. Since it was already paid for and nonrefundable, I had decided to go and be with my daughter who had been on the same emotional roller coaster. We could both sit together in silence and relax. Plus, the place we chose was beautiful, right along the water. I figured that the smell of the salt water, the gentle breezes, the sunshine, clear blue skies, and dining at great restaurants by the sea was exactly what was needed to calm my frayed nerves.

It was our first morning there, and the mood was somber until her husband texted me the song "I Will Survive" by Gloria Gaynor. Listening to the words that exactly tapped into what I was feeling, my eyes welled with tears. I had spent so many nights wondering what I had done wrong for "him doing me wrong." As I focused on the lyrics, the song helped me not only identify what I was feeling but empowered me to not crumble and fall apart. I was determined to "change that stupid lock on the door, tell him to turn around and walk back out when he came again with that sad look upon (his) face."

I was petrified, but I still had a life to live.

How many times have I allowed him to cruelly manipulate as if I were nothing? How often have I said something but was muzzled with criticism? How many times have I suppressed my feelings as if they didn't matter? How often have I showed up for things that didn't bring me much joy but did it anyway to please? And why have I put up with feeling uncomfortable around behavior that didn't match my values? How in the world did I never notice this before?

My brain was shifting, similar to a kaleidoscope twisting and creating a different image with the same pieces.

I was seeing things I couldn't see before and just now understood the counselor's mysterious laugh... and I could feel courage rising. Courage to let go of shame that didn't belong to me. Courage to withstand his scorn. Courage to shrug off the judgment of others.

I can survive this!

But still, there was uncertainty and doubt. Survival meant a new beginning, a new way of life, a transition I never wanted.

I have nothing to prove anymore. I can't control what others think of me so why do I feel obligated to change me? They can be on their own soul's journey... with me on mine.

Without needing approval from anyone, I remembered Nike's motto "Just Do It." I wanted to just deal with shame without shaming. I wanted to just let go the lie that others are better-than and allow myself to feel deserving of honest and loving relationships. I wanted to just live my life according to my values and be able to breathe, relax, and just be.

As I sat there, breathing in the fresh air of St. Maarten, listening to Gloria, and feeling my spirits lift, something else shifted in me. Noticing how the music helped promote strength made me think of all the incredible research I'd been doing on light and sound.

Seeing the Invisible

Physicist Albert Einstein described humanity as "energetic beings in physical form—slowed down *light* and *sound* frequencies." Our physical skin suit is literally made when both *light* and *sound* arrange four atoms together to create a human cell. Every organ in the body is affected by *light* and *sound* because every organ is made of cells—which are created by *light* and *sound.* Every cell has a vibrational frequency at its core.

Why does this matter?

While we are not the Source of light, we're *always* connected to it. Our cells send and receive photons back and forth all day long; and the bloodstream, 75% percent of which is *water*, is like a river of light running through the body. Just as harnessing electricity changed the world when we learned how to harness its power, when we learn how to harness light within, it can affect how we perceive the world around us—how we think, how we feel and how we relate to one another.

As top neuroscientists now know—it isn't what we "think" that creates our future. It's how we FEEL. Why? The majority of our thoughts are held in the subconscious. Dr. Masaru Emoto published a book in 2004 after experiments designed to show the effects of this new field of Quantum energy on water. He exposed several glasses of water to different vibrational frequencies, or tones. After each exposure, the water was frozen and sliced into thin sections to view under a microscope. The results were incredible. Tones that sounded soft and loving formed beautiful, snowflake-like, geometric structures, whereas tones that sounded harsh and angry left no structure at all. (For a visual, check out his experiments on YouTube.)

As cells swim in the energetic river, photons cross the cell's membrane to reach DNA. The more light allowed in, the more cells feel good. In fact, the amount of light allowed in depends on how open or closed cells are, which determines mental and physical health.

What determines how open or closed our cells are? Our emotional state.

Cells are smart. Designed to operate like a battery, they will either have a positive, negative, or neutral response to stimuli given to our five senses. Scientists created a human Richter scale over a twenty-year span wherein millions of different pictures, music, scents, tastes, and things to touch were observed, measured, and recorded. There was a neutral, zero charge, when provided soothing sounds like childhood melodies, pictures of holding a newborn, or an experience of someone filled with gratitude. At lower hertz levels, *thoughts* correlated to guilt, shame, anger, and jealousy. Faster frequencies correlated to more pleasurable *thoughts*, such as fun, love, joy, and peace.

Each emotion carries a specific speed and wavelength that can be measured with EKG and EEG machines. When angry, wavelengths spike and get erratic. When calm, wavelengths have a rhythmic beat. Natural, smooth, rhythmic beats occur when thoughts align with heart qualities. Scientists have other equipment that show the impact of emotions on the brain. Our brains light up (literally with sparks) when we tune into the activities that are playful and fun. They dim down when activities are boring and monotonous.

When thankful, the electrical circuit of the cell is complete or "grounded" and forms those crystalline shapes like we see in Dr. Masaru Emoto's experiment, which are known to prevent cell damage and help them stay connected and supporting one another. In contrast, when anger and other lower vibrations course through our veins, these low, heavy sounds are slow and dense and cause cells to contract and fold over to self-preserve—meaning light can't reach the DNA to provide energy, stay connected, and support one another.

Emotions are what determine whether my cells are open or closed and how much light is able to infuse my cells. If my emotions are the determining factor here, and my emotions are generated by my thoughts, and I get to choose what I think about and focus on,

then ultimately, I am responsible for whether my cells are open or closed—whether I'm thriving or merely surviving.

That's why this song lifted my mood so quickly and effortlessly. And, as my cells began attuning to a higher frequency, my mind became more open to accept what happened and move on with a "Just do it!" attitude.

I decided to ask others to send me songs they thought would be helpful. It was a wonderful experience to receive them and experience the regular uplifting of my spirit. It also gave me insight into others' ideas of how they would respond if they had to go through a similar experience. My playlist today is a reminder of how many "old and new" friends were willing to come along side during a time when I felt so betrayed, isolated, and alone. Their love and acceptance confirmed the transformative power of love and the benefit of having others support and encourage with empathy—very different than sympathy.

Sympathy vs. Empathy

Sympathy involves pity and sorrow
for someone's misfortune.

Empathy identifies with an emotion and
makes someone feel seen and heard.

Downward Spirals

DNA is a spiral, always spiraling upward, for more growth and expansion. Adventure, with all its danger, is a deep longing within our DNA. But not all thoughts spiral upward.

The fear of losing my marriage, something so loved, produced an incredible ache as thoughts spiraled DNA downward with emotions of anger, fear, guilt, and shame. Pain is normal when facing the loss of love. But pain is also the opposite direction of growth and expansion. When emotions go unresolved, it results in chronic stress—the #1 reason for chronic diseases. Even though it might be a low-grade stress, not the acute and intense as a sudden breach of trust, ongoing stress seeps harmful chemicals into the bloodstream to bring the body back into balance and keep organs working efficiently.

Well-documented research shows that chronic stress sets off a vicious cycle. The release of adrenaline and cortisol to manage stress slows down organs. A slower digestive system leads to weight gain, obesity and diabetes. Extra adrenaline contributes to lack of sleep which raises stress hormones even more. The immune system gets overwhelmed and can't easily fight off infections. Living in a state of chronic stress teeters mental and physical health. Unless interrupted, the cycle repeats over and over. One traumatic event can push us over the edge.

All of that chronic stress took its toll on my body, I thought to myself as I reflected on this research. I couldn't help but think of the state of low-level anxiety I had lived with all my life resulting from the stress of always trying to please others. All my choices were affected and now I understood they affected my cells as well. *This has got to be at least partly responsible for the breast cancer I beat five years ago!*

It has been proven that the fate of the cell is not determined by genes. We inherit genes, but they can remain unexpressed. Expression depends on what the organ needs to stay healthy. When the quality of energy is substandard, cells suffer and a gene is triggered to help out. In other words, the quality of fuel is what determines the cell's health—which includes the quality of our thoughts, sleep, nutrition, exercise, what we're exposed to in the environment, relationships and more.

Prior to my diagnosis, I owned/managed a fast-food restaurant in the food court of a mall. Even though the original intent was for us to only be investors, I ended up having to quit my job in the medical field to manage it. Managing a restaurant, when I had never even worked in one, and dealing with the constant turnover of irresponsible teen employees was incredibly stressful—a commitment well beyond what I had ever anticipated or wanted. In truth, an entire book could be written about all the crazymaking I experienced.

When approached by mall owners to expand one store to three, I immediately said, "NO!" I didn't want to manage people and didn't want the time commitment this business required. When my husband kept insisting, making comments such as "How hard can fast food be? It's not rocket science," I was so hurt that he didn't recognize my hard work and sacrifice. He persisted, repeatedly ignoring my "no," and I eventually felt guilty for not wanting "the great opportunity" he wanted. His persistence and my guilt convinced me to "give in." Another decade was spent trying to keep two more stores afloat. The stress didn't just triple. It increased exponentially. We ended up losing one store and going through a major court battle with the other.

And then, within a month after they sold, we moved... away from the family and friends I wanted to spend more time with... so that he could have a third career. Within a few short months, I was diagnosed with cancer.

I knew stress was an issue in health, but never fully connected it to my cancer until I found out in my research that in 1979, Dr. Ryke Hamer discovered he had cancer only three months after his seventeen-year-old son was tragically shot and killed. Realizing that his cancer must have had something to do with the loss of his son, he went on to prove that every so called "disease" is caused by ongoing "dis-ease" in the body. Disease is a biological response meant to facilitate conflict resolution. The body knows how to heal itself but when stressed long term a natural rhythm becomes unnatural. As cells remain out of balance, pain emerges for the individual's greatest chance of survival. In other words, pain is an act of self-love built into our system.

Thank goodness I'm learning how to step out of this crazy loop!

The Narcissist's Chemical Loop

When recovering from narcissistic abuse, it's important to take this conversation one step further. The way a manipulator keeps us hooked is by alternating between two very powerful emotions: fear and love. Narcissists look forward to the catch, not the person. Similar to a cat waiting for a mouse to come out of its hiding place, a narcissist will appear safe and trustworthy in a phase known as Love-bombing (feels like love), which produces oxytocin (a hormone known to increase the desire to draw near and increase bonding). During this phase they're "present," appear interested, watch closely and listen intently. However, it is only to find ways to pounce later. When they find the right moment, they go into the Devalue phase and bat emotions around (feels like fear), which produces cortisol (a hormone that creates the desire to fight, freeze or pull away).

These two opposing systems in the body (parasympathetic and sympathetic) respond in the same way that a football team uses both defense and offense to win the game. A manipulator thinks their job in the game of "who's in control" is to keep us on the defense by "motivating" with charming but fake moves. The more successful their manipulative tactics are at getting us to sympathize and "give in," the more they'll use them again and again as a way to solve their problems. Psychology researchers call this back-and-forth treatment "intermittent reinforcement." It is known to be highly addictive—the most powerful motivator on the planet.

This cycle of feeling love and then fearing the loss of it, creates what's known as a "trauma bond." Trauma bonds are similar to the Stockholm Syndrome, the psychological coping mechanism noticed when a captive, tied to a chair and gagged, not knowing their future and in a state of intense fear, suddenly experiences their captor acting really nice and bringing them a meal. There's incredible relief and the hope of being set free. Powerful chemicals of relief and hope... after fear... can create intense bonding that feels like love. In fact, many captives have been known to marry their captors, all because of a chemical reaction within the body.

A skilled manipulator begins utilizing tactics so insidiously that we won't notice it for what it is while it's happening... unless we are aware of the tactics and the predictable cycle.

In my case, he would speak in a convincing, soothing voice, bring flowers, and write sweet cards. It lowered my defenses and created intense bonding which left me vulnerable to suggestion. Whenever he stonewalled, didn't show up, or "forgot" to do something he had promised to do, he demeaned my normal reaction (emotions) and convinced me that I was somehow responsible. My naivete and overly conscientious mind were all-too-ready to see his side of things and all-too-willing to blame myself. Instead of recognizing that he was fighting to have control, I ignored my feelings and tried to understand and find valid reasons for his behavior.

No one had told me that the first rule to follow when made to feel guilty for someone else's broken promise or poor behavior is: *Do not listen to any explanation!*

The Narcissist's rationale is totally irrelevant. Even though it may not have been intentional, it is their responsibility to apologize and explain what they will do to not allow it to happen again.

Unfortunately, once taught to consider emotions irrelevant, it becomes natural to invalidate them. Our only recourse is to lean on the mind's intellect and not on our body's intuitive and instinctual knowing. Once access to that feedback has been taken away, it's easy to become dependent on someone else to validate our worth. And, it makes it much easier for us to be exploited and manipulated by someone resisting submission to the basic principles of civil conduct.

Many of us Codependents martyr ourselves on the altar of virtue while the Narcissist takes advantage of our virtues—the greatest assets we have to offer. The oxytocin-cortisol loop motivates us to think, feel, and behave the way the Narcissist wants us to think, feel, and behave. In the bad times, we learn to be patient and wait for the good times to return. This is usually a familiar childhood coping mechanism for those of us who had to keep looking for moments of safety in an unpredictable home.

Looking back, I can see things I couldn't see then. Truth is, I wasn't even looking—so, of course, I totally missed it. It simply never occurred to me that he could be lying or using other passive aggressive tactics. It never entered my mind to mistrust his motives. My tendency was to mistrust mine and trust his, serve, and make his life pleasurable. Unfortunately, that only worked until I got so frustrated that I blew up, which is the manipulator's goal. Once I lost it, he could point out my misbehavior and make me feel guilty for it, distracting my attention from his wrongdoing.

While emotions are a natural aspect of the human experience, they can be so overpowering and cause humans to do and say things completely out of character. It doesn't matter how sound your thinking is. You can't think well in the absence of love. Whenever I did get angry, it didn't feel *right* to stay angry; therefore, I chose to adjust and adapt, or overlook his behavior and attacks on my motives and memory. I "gave in" so often that I became emotionally numb to slights and insults. We rarely argued. As long as I believed his excuses and defaulted to what he wanted, things were fine. However, when it came to the affair, I was adamant with my "no" and refused to give in.

I was stunned silent when my counselor said it was most likely the first time I had ever stood my ground with him.

No way! I looked at her as if she were crazy. *I'm pretty certain I've been making my own decisions with my own free will.* And, then she asked me to think of a time when I got my way.

More silence. I couldn't come up with one single instance.

You mean, even though I thought I was acting on my own free will, I was actually being manipulated with guilt and shame to make the choices he wanted me to make?!?

The realization of this truth made me livid for days.

Barely Escaping the Loop

Armed with this understanding, I knew I had to stop falling prey to these tactics that can cause the "nicest" person in the world to lose it and want to throw something out the window. I was a victim of lies but still had choices about what I did with those lies. I saw myself through the lens of unworthiness, knew my role and knew I had to take responsibility for all my past choices. After all, staying angry does a number on the immune system. As Stephen Covey, author of *The 7 Habits of Highly Effective People,* notes, "Until you are able to say, 'I am what I am today because of the choices I made yesterday,' you cannot say, 'I choose otherwise.'"

Unfortunately, what I quickly realized is that even though I knew the facts of what was going on, my brain was still addicted to the "intermittent reinforcement" of the chemical loop, leading me to plead with him to stay and work together to have the good times return. They say this addiction is as bad as heroine, and I can certainly vouch for that.

During the week in St. Maarten, and for several months after, my body literally ached to call and see how he was doing. Even though I had just caught him at her house, I would have called in a heartbeat had it not been for poor cell phone coverage on the island. Back home, I reverted to my old, comfy patterns *many* times. Once, when they were on a camping trip together, I wanted to know how he was doing and craved calling to see whether he was enjoying himself at the places *we* once camped together. I wasn't even making sense to myself.

Why would I want to know whether he was having fun with her? And why would I want to stay in a marriage with someone so willing to break every marital vow, disrespect himself, and me?

As a Codependent, knowing I couldn't "fix things" made me feel incredibly helpless. My new goal was to make sound choices on my behalf, independent of what he, or others, chose. This meant noticing emotions as one of my top goals and reminding myself that there will always be those who enjoy pulling the wool over our eyes for their own level of entertainment. The more in control we are over how we respond to their idea of fun, the more drama we can avoid and the more peace of mind we can hope to experience. I had no control over any-one's choices but my own, and my focus had to be on my own behavior and how I had been *mistreating myself*. I couldn't do this if I continued to focus on what he was doing.

They say we can actually miss someone emotionally abusing us as much as someone misses alcohol. So true.

To beat the addiction, I had to force myself to put down the phone, delete carefully worded texts, and stop trying "one more time." Each time my body curled in pain, I had to remind myself that his behavior was about his own internal circuitry, and my behavior was about mine. This certainly made it much easier to take his comments less personally, leaving me with more energy to deal with my own pattern of trying to control by pleading, arguing, or negotiating.

Goal: Reverse-Engineering My Loop

The good news is that the brain can be rewired pretty quickly, simply with reverse-engineering.

Childhood programming caused me to consider others "more worthy." To rewire my brain, I reverse-engineered and paid attention to any emotion that made me feel "less worthy." Rather than fight emotions off, I welcomed them and rode them like an ocean wave until they passed.

They say about a third of our neurons can be rewired in just one week. Which means, if consistent, it'd take about three weeks to break a habit. However, because I spent decades judging emotions as wrong, it made it hard for me to resist the urge to push them below the surface again. It took about eighteen months to recover and then reinforce and strengthen my new habit.

Unlike the butterfly that transforms seamlessly, nothing about my transformation was seamless. Was it a simple process? Yes. Easy? Absolutely not. It felt incredibly unloving to not help. To let him experience the consequences of his own choices, knowing there would be consequences for me and my family, came with a lot of pent-up tears—a *healthy* way to release desperate, hopeless, helpless feelings.

And yet, nothing is more powerful than a made-up mind.

Step 1: Tune Out the Lies

I decided ahead of time that I would not "play" the next time I was lured into a power struggle. Listening is crucial in communication, but Narcissists don't really listen. They listen only to be keenly aware of what the Codependent values, so they know what to devalue later. They're more like a boxer in the ring, ready to come out and fight. They know exactly when to attack good-hearted motives with unwarranted criticism so that we'll try to fight back and defend ourselves. They know how to twist words (known as word salad), what stories to make up, and what qualities to criticize. I learned the hard way that defense is never a good position to take in a Narcissistic/Codependent relationship. Inevitably I would become adamant or outraged, drawing attention away from his misbehavior; and suddenly, I was the problem.

I couldn't go down that road again.

To tune into the subconscious world of my inner thoughts, I paid attention to any remark that triggered a reaction. Each reaction represented an app downloaded during childhood to keep me safe from harm. My brain did a really good job figuring out how to survive, but some of those apps weren't necessary anymore. To recognize fear and stare it down, I had to trust that my body was telling me the truth. I noticed how quickly a defense bubbled up when words were twisted, how frustrated I got when criticized for asking a simple question, and how fast I made excuses and stepped in to fix things when a simple request was ignored. I faced every fear, stayed the course, and rode every wave of guilt and shame until it passed.

As usual, he wasn't making good on any of his promises. Instead, he vacillated between the use of love and fear. One minute he'd compliment my efforts to please, and I'd think all was well; and the next minute he'd claim the most benign comment was out-of-line. I'd respond one minute and react the next. It shook my nerves and rattled my brain, yet he had a smirk on his face as if he were having great balls of fun. I had no clue how things would work out in the future, but I refused to be the damsel in distress anymore continually "giving in" for his gain and my loss of self.

The rule of thumb when dealing with a skilled manipulator is to have them follow through with what they say they'll do... *first...* before doing or giving anything in return. They love to come back later with comments such as "I never said that," when we know they did. They know exactly how to make comments in a calm and logical way so that we get flustered and doubt our logic.

Gaslighting is a hallmark for Narcissists. The term comes from the 1944 film *Gaslight* where a husband kept turning down the lights in the room. When the wife mentioned how the room seemed darker, he made her think it was her eyesight, not the fact that he had turned the lights down.

Gaslighting is a form of psychological abuse where a person manipulates the truth to make someone question their sanity, perception of reality, or memory. People experiencing gaslighting often feel confused, anxious, and unable to trust themselves.

For example, we would agree to do chores on the weekend, even go so far as to decide the amount of time we would spend on them; and then when the weekend came, I would hear, "I don't know what you're talking about. I never said that. You knew I had other plans." It left my head spinning, trying to recall the conversation. I would often repeat it verbatim, and he would deny it over and over until I finally said, "Never mind, let's just forget it."

My new goal was to not be manipulated, and he immediately tested my resolve.

I let him know that I would never be able to trust him again unless he sought counsel. He said he would seek counsel if I would allow him to come home… to see if he could trust me. It was tempting. I wanted him home and I didn't want to lose my marriage. However, it was another bait-and-switch tactic—another attempt to make me feel responsible and guilty for the separation. He knew how important marriage was for me. He was tapping into my fear of losing it, and I knew it. I also knew he had a track record of never following through with what he said. In fact, when I stood firm that he seek counsel first, he flipped the conversation around to say he wouldn't come back until I got counseling. The fact was, I was already in counseling; but he kept insisting, telling everyone I had anger issues and refused to get the help I so badly needed.

As the one who wanted to be accurate with truth, it was hard to step back and not speak to the facts. I was being blamed for things he was doing, and they were things I wouldn't even think of doing. I had to learn to not take the bait. I also had to tune out those who believed what he was saying was true.

Struggling with the intense anger I felt when others wanted me to be a good Christian by "humbling" myself and "offering forgiveness," I was beginning to think *Maybe I do have anger issues?!?* To be viewed as not embodying the Christian persona was my worst fear ever.

"It is taking all my strength to stay the course and not be bullied into doing what he wants me to do; and now this person on the other end of the line is telling *me* I need to humble *myself*, forgive, and be a good Christian? I wanted to throw the frickin' phone out the window," I angrily confessed to my counselor.

"I probably would have done it." She gently smiled back.

Her lighthearted comment made me laugh, and I realized how harshly I was treating myself. *Why wouldn't I be angry with someone lying, twisting words, slandering, and blame-shifting?*

When others respond with their limited understanding of the full story, it is known in the psych world as "secondary abuse."

I was so done with all of it and decided I needed to just allow everyone to be who they needed to be—and not who I *wanted* them to be. I did everything I could out of love for my husband, was there for him every step of the way… but I'd never taken steps to be there for myself. It was time to be on my own team and let go of the desire to explain or have others understand me.

I was enough.

Step 2: Let Go
Alarming statistics show that 1 in 5 fall into this category of narcissism, and only 5% of these are willing to change. Thus, we have what appears to be an epidemic in our culture, and

traditional once-a-week counseling is a waste of time and money. What has been successful is a more intense recovery program. I was made aware of the Marriage Recovery Center in Bainbridge, Washington. Having dealt with this personality long enough, the staff are experts at determining whether the Narcissist is willing to stick to the program long enough to retrain the brain. Most Narcissists tend to quit when the counselor tries to hold them accountable.

As a part of my "letting go" process, I decided to offer my husband the program by being direct and to the point. Since Narcissists consider emotions to be immature and absurd, they don't respond to any type of emotional plea. For instance, I couldn't say, in a little girl's pleading voice, "Pretty please, for the sake of our family, will you try this program?" Instead, I said, in a low, matter-of-fact voice, "If you're interested in trying it, my counselor says this is a great program." Then I left the ball in his court to make the first move.

Circumstances never changed. He completely dismissed the offer, and I refused to repeatedly offer the program or budge from my value of a marriage based on fidelity.

The heart has its own brain. It's an electrical organ with its own vessels and nervous system and vibrates at a higher frequency in comparison to the other organs. And somehow my heart felt lighter to not fight for what I wanted anymore. The "new me" was living inside-out, honoring my values with my values. The "old me" was living outside-in, saying, "Honor me! Don't you want to leave a legacy for the kids? Don't you appreciate all my efforts to please you? Don't you remember all the fun times we had together? Please say *yes*!" It was extremely painful to admit that four decades of offering love and support to fulfill his dreams meant absolutely nothing to him.

Then suddenly fear came roaring back. *"Maybe he does love me and is teachable. Maybe I can try one more time."* Surprisingly, I had to wrestle with these thoughts repeatedly.

My kids were grown, and my mom role already looked very different. Many of my friends lived in other states. These were the retirement years I'd been looking forward to forever. I had never lived alone. The future was unknown, and I kept asking myself questions with unknown answers. *What will I do with my life when my wife role is gone? Who will I have fun with? Will I have any friends left? Will anyone care?*

As scary as it was, I was determined to let go of my role as a Codependent. The definition of insanity is to repeat the same thing over and over, expecting different results. What's the point of a relationship if it can't be trusted? Of course, I really didn't have a choice. He was already separating our accounts and asking me to make a list to divide our assets.

Step 3: Add Forgiveness

To move on, I first had to offer myself forgiveness for not knowing any better. I had to come to terms with the fact that not only was I angry at him, I was angry at the entire culture for considering emotions irrelevant. The rules we have followed as a society made no sense and "truth" led to so much physical and mental pain. We followed them without question which allowed me, my parents and grandparents and so many others, to be emotionally abused. And yet, forgiving every-one, including myself, was necessary to avoid creating more abuse. It made it easier when I realized there is only a certain amount of storage in my computer-brain. If space is taken up with anger, there's no room left to create anything new. Also, understanding I was naïve, doing the best I knew to do, I imagined everyone might be naïve, doing the best with what they know to do.

When we choose to forgive, it doesn't mean we wipe away or forget what someone did. And it doesn't mean that the person isn't accountable for their actions either. Forgiveness simply means releasing anger and refusing retaliation. It kicks in the parasympathetic system, relaxes cells, and keeps the mind open to look for new ideas and ways to relate.

> **Forgiveness** is the choice to let go of anger and resentment towards yourself or someone else.
> It's a decision to let go any thoughts of revenge and to move forward with your personal power intact.
>
> **Accountability** is about accepting responsibility for one's actions.

A New Creature

At the next session with my counselor, I told her about the continued blame-shifting and refusal to seek counsel.

She looked at me with sorrow and said, "What do you want to do? He can't give you honesty right now," and proceeded to point to the facts.

At the end of our session, she suggested I attend a Divorce Care class. I knew she was right, but it felt like defeat, as if I should hold on just a little bit longer. I grabbed a Kleenex, nodded, and agreed.

When I showed up for the first class, I went up four steps of the staircase and back down at least half a dozen times before someone stopped me and asked if I needed help. The kind volunteer guided me to the room. I didn't want to be there. I wanted to wake up from a bad dream and have this entire nightmare go away.

This is so unfair, and I shouldn't have to be doing this, I thought as I felt frustration, shame and anger all over again. *Will these feelings ever go away?* I wondered and realized that being overly-conscientious can be a good thing, too. I didn't want to tell my counselor I didn't go when I said I would. While I knew it was time to end things and get off the emotional roller coaster, it didn't make the process any easier.

The leaders knew how we felt. They had been there/done that, too, and had a lot of empathy. The first session was learning what to expect from the program. We would watch a film and have time to talk after. After several weeks of listening to personal stories and acclimating to the fact that this was reality, the movies began. They were good, providing more facts that were helpful. However, the conversation that followed was a litany of "he said/she said" comments that shamed and blamed the other. It was not only draining, but I knew from my research that neurological ruts were going deeper and would only add more suffering to what was already painful. After each class, I left the room totally frustrated, physically and emotionally drained. I convinced myself to finish the class by treating myself to a Dunkin Donut on my way home—just for showing up.

Another program serendipitously showed up while I was on my computer one day. On a whim, I decided to spend the money, sign up, and try it. It was a weekend-long program designed to deal with toxic relationships without becoming toxic yourself. It felt like a breath of fresh air. I was introduced to several speakers very aware of the quantum field and who knew how to move the energy of grief through the body in a healthy way.

When D-Day finally came, I was ready for the ride. I watched my husband enter the courtroom lighthearted and making jokes with our lawyer-friend. My lawyer was busy with something that needed to be handled, so I sat on a bench in the back of the courtroom alone, my stomach in knots. I couldn't believe I *still* held a tiny glimmer of hope he would change his mind. He caught my eye for what seemed like an eternity and stared at me as if wanting me to crumble. I stared back with an unflinching look. The stare broke when the judge entered, looked at the papers, and asked him one question: "Do you really think your marriage is over?"

He answered soberly with a quiet "Yes," as if he were so disappointed.

The gavel came down and just like that, what I thought would last forever ended. I did want to crumble. I knew this day was coming, but it felt like half of me was being ripped away. Having been married over four decades, there were so many memories. I had enjoyed serving his needs and helping him reach his goals. I knew the way he walked, the way he held and kissed my face, what he liked to eat, and what he said at night just before we went to sleep. There would be no more late-night conversations, no more running jokes, no more texting many times a day to see how he was doing. My role as wife just ended, my "married" label was gone, and all my hopes and dreams of living together 'til death do us part just died. It was difficult for me to keep it together.

I quickly texted the kids, "It's done," and got up to leave the courtroom. As I walked out the door, I remembered the banner I had made for our wedding day: "We're on the Brink of Heaven Knows What Discoveries." Little did I know the words chosen more than four decades ago would mean that the end of one relationship would be the discovery of a new one—the one I have with myself. I left the courtroom feeling defeated but proud of myself for standing up for what I truly valued. I even walked out the door with a glimmer of hope, curious as to what was in store for the next chapter of my life.

When I went to the parking garage, I discovered I needed cash to get out.

Seriously? Who carries cash these days? I fumbled for money in my purse. Nerve-wracked from the weight of the morning's experiences, I couldn't think straight, couldn't find any money, and couldn't think of any options. While trying really hard to concentrate, I saw my new "ex" of ten minutes and our lawyer-friend walking toward the garage.

Can this day be any more traumatizing?

As they entered the garage his lawyer looked at me kindly. *He is a good guy,* I reminded myself as an important memory from the morning flashed through my mind. When my husband had slipped out of the courtroom, he had come over to me to apologize for ever getting involved.

When I asked him if I could borrow some money, he took my ticket and paid for it.

"Thank you," I said. "Can you put it on his tab?" I smiled and pointed to my ex, who gave me a weak smile back while his lawyer handed me the paid stub.

I couldn't remember where I parked the car and walked up and down the ramps of the parking lot looking for it. When I finally found it, I sat there numb just staring straight ahead for heaven knows how long. Finally, a car next to me started which snapped me out of the trance. I left the garage, drove home, entered my quiet house, and began living alone for the very first time ever.

Music Playlist

1. I Will Survive ~ Gloria Gaynor
2. I Am... I Said ~ Neil Diamond
3. Song Of My Father ~ Urban Rescue
4. Fight Song ~ Rachel Platten
5. Overcomer ~ Mandisa
6. Stand ~ Rascal Flatts
7. Brave ~ Sara Bereilles
8. Anchor Me ~ The Tenors
9. Heartlight ~ Neil Diamond
10. Be Still My Soul ~ Selah
11. Oh Fear ~ Moriah Peters
12. I Am Not Alone ~ Kari Jobe
13. Tell Your Heart To Beat Again ~ Danny Gokey
14. May I Suggest ~ Red Molly
15. For Good ~ Kristin Chenoweth
16. The Greatest Love of All ~ Whitney Houston
17. How We Love ~ Beth Nielsen Chapman
18. The Rose ~ Bette Midler
19. You Can Do This Hard Thing ~ Carrie Newcomer
20. Voice of Truth ~ Casting Crowns
21. One Small Voice ~ Carole King
22. Never Once ~ Matt Redman
23. Right on Time ~ Brandi Carlile
24. She Let Herself Go ~ George Strait
25. Blessings ~ Laura Story
26. Headed for the Future ~ Neil Diamond
27. Rise Up ~ Andra Day

CHAPTER FOUR
Developing Faith in Your Wings

Discovering that God/Life Supports You and Believes You are Worthy

"To fear love is to fear life and those who
fear life are already three parts dead."

~ Bertrand Russell ~

I made one last appointment with my counselor to thank her for being so helpful. She had been such a great listener and confidante that it was hard to put an end to my sessions. However, counseling was a generous gift given by the church; and since my divorce was over, I knew it was time to give my space to another.

Before my appointment, I knew I needed another listening ear. I couldn't share my grief with my kids. They were grieving the loss of an intact family. I couldn't share my grief with my siblings either. They were grieving, too. Friends freely gave me sympathy, but I didn't want sympathy. I didn't want anyone giving me advice on how to move on either. I just needed someone to listen.

JOIN US AT CAMP DO GOOD. *Give Blood.*

American Red Cross

Make an appointment to donate blood at one of these convenient locations. Find more at RedCrossBlood.org or on the Blood Donor App.

Hyperion Materials & Technologies
Tuesday, June 27, 2023
10:30 AM to 4:30 PM
6325 Huntley Road
Columbus, OH, 43229
Call 1-800-RED CROSS (1-800-733-2767) to schedule your appointment or search online for sponsor code: Hyperion
Give in June for a $10 gift card by email plus chance to win home theater package.
rcblood.org/June

Worthington Education Association
Tuesday, June 13, 2023
11:30 AM to 5:30 PM
200 East Wilson Bridge Road
Worthington, OH, 43085
Call 1-800-RED CROSS (1-800-733-2767) to schedule your appointment or search online for sponsor code: WEA
Give in June for a $10 gift card by email plus chance to win home theater package.
rcblood.org/June

Cott Systems
Tuesday, June 13, 2023
10:00 AM to 4:00 PM
2800 Corporate Exchange Drive
Columbus, OH, 43231
Call Eric Payne at (800) 234-2699 to schedule your appointment or search online for sponsor code: cott
Give in June for a $10 gift card by email plus chance to win home theater package.
rcblood.org/June

AAA Ohio Auto Club
Wednesday, June 21, 2023
10:00 AM to 4:00 PM
at Ohio Auto Club
90 E. Wilson Bridge Rd.
Worthington, OH, 43085
Call Annie Ackley at (614) 431-7859 to schedule your appointment or search online for sponsor code: AutoClubOH
Give in June for a $10 gift card by email plus chance to win home theater package. rcblood.org/June

Worthington Presbyterian Church
Monday, June 12, 2023
11:30 AM to 5:30 PM
773 High Street
Worthington, OH, 43085
Call 1-800-RED CROSS (1-800-733-2767) to schedule your appointment or search online for sponsor code: Worthpres
Give in June for a $10 gift card by email plus chance to win home theater package.
rcblood.org/June

Congregation Beth Tikvah
Tuesday, June 27, 2023
12:00 PM to 6:00 PM
6121 Olentangy River Road
Worthington, OH, 43085
Call 1-800-RED CROSS (1-800-733-2767) to schedule your appointment or search online for sponsor code: bethtikvah
Give in June for a $10 gift card by email plus chance to win home theater package.
rcblood.org/June

Alexander,

We're reminiscing about summer camp days of youth. Whether you were a camper, counselor or just enjoyed classic summer camp flicks, we invite you to reconnect with those simpler times with us. Channel those nostalgic I-can-do-anything feelings to help make a difference this summer: **Join Camp Do Good and give blood!**

This time of year, the need for blood gets in-TENTS. We need donors like you to pitch in and help by scheduling a donation appointment today! You'll be a happy camper knowing your donation may help save more than one life.

No matter where you are, Camp Do Good is calling! Embrace the excitement of camp and make a commitment to donate blood as often as you're eligible this summer. **Good things happen when you give!**

SCHEDULE YOUR APPOINTMENT TODAY!

Download the Blood Donor App | RedCrossBlood.org
1-800-RED CROSS (1-800-733-2767)
Enable the Blood Donor Skill for Alexa Echo devices

If you have recently made a donation, already scheduled an appointment or been told previously by the Red Cross or another blood center that you should never donate blood, please disregard this message. To confirm your eligibility to donate, please call 1-800-RED CROSS (1-800-733-2767). Times and locations subject to change.
© The American National Red Cross | 2023-APL-0201 | Calendar ID 2027789 | 383701-01-Generic-RW

Check your vitals!

Track your blood pressure, hemoglobin and pulse in your online profile.
RedCrossBlood.org/HealthAssessment

American Red Cross

Blood Services
405 West John H. Gwynn Jr. Ave.
Peoria, IL 61605

```
*****************AUTO**ALL FOR AADC 430 - 8856 - T29
4C20826                              051523-SEAS-6
Alexander Intres
1446 Norma Rd
Columbus OH 43229-5118
```

Non Profit Org
U.S. Postage
PAID
American
Red Cross

I set the intention and paid attention. My new approach was to ask for the "what," not the "how," and watch for an answer. Now that I was aware of the mind-body connection, I knew that to find solutions, cells had to be open and relaxed to have my mind open to see opportunities. I couldn't believe how fast it worked.

One morning, after I threw out the request, the first thought to cross my mind was to take a walk. It seemed like a lighthearted, good idea—an easy decision. I put on my walking gear and went to the park. I was listening to music when a gal stopped me along the trail.

I bet she lost her dog, I thought as I took my earbuds out to hear what she was saying.

"You look like someone I know," she said.

"Who?" I asked.

She named my sister. We had a short five-minute conversation about how the two of them knew each other. At the end, she said, "Hey, I'm beginning a small prayer group in a few weeks. Would you like to join us?"

"Thanks. Let me think about it!" I responded quickly. My new first go-to response was to give myself time to decide whether things felt open and relaxed or closed and constrictive—rather than defaulting to my habit of always saying "yes" when I really wanted to say "no." I was becoming more familiar with internal thoughts (emotions) that drove my choices and was determined to leave my pattern of people-pleasing. As I continued walking, I wasn't sure I wanted to go. She was friendly and the invitation felt genuine, but the thought of studying or sharing my newly-divorced status with a group of strangers made me cringe. I wanted one person, not many. Plus, the invitation came within a half hour of my request, making me think it couldn't possibly be the answer. I decided to let the invitation go.

Two days later, I was on the same trail when I ran into her again. This time, she was with another gal who seemed to be my daughter's age. After another short five-minute conversation, she also mentioned the new group and asked me if I would be interested.

"Thanks, let me think about it," I repeated, hesitant to commit on the spot.

As I returned to my walk, I thought it was so uncanny to meet the same person twice in a week on a random walk at the park. I wondered why I was feeling nervous about saying "yes" and realized it was because I was feeling uncertain about what I would do if I didn't like it.

If I don't like the group, how do I leave? I do not want to feel obligated, and I don't want them to feel bad. Omg, my "people-pleasing" habit, I thought when I noticed it.

I finished the walk, deciding how I would exit gracefully if I went and the group wasn't the right fit. The Nike motto "just do it" came to mind again. It felt like such a simple solution to what now seemed a stupid problem, but my ongoing habit of pleasing others had been crystalized in my nervous system for decades.

Come on, Kathleen, I coached myself. *You're trying to control what people think, and it's impossible. It's NOT selfish to honor your feelings and discern whether others are a good match. It's perfectly healthy. Don't trample on yourself. Change the pattern! Let the fear go!*

I chuckled and chided myself at the same time and wondered how to get in touch with one of the gals I just met.

Later that afternoon, I was checking emails and an invitation popped up from the place they would be meeting. *Wow, that was fast!* I was so surprised but knew immediately to hit the return button with a "yes." I still wondered if I would like the group but felt more confident in saying "Not for me, thank you." Plus, with three offers in three days, I didn't want to strike out on the third attempt for God to get my attention.

The group ended up being a perfect fit. We met weekly in a small, inviting room with a small round table. The middle of the table held a lit candle, representing the light of Christ. The meeting began with a chosen reading and sometimes music to set the mood. Each participant then took turns speaking to what they were "present to" while the others would "hold space." The rules were simple. No crosstalk. No "fixing." No judging. We were merely there to listen and allow each to hear their own voice. The belief at the core of these rules was that, bearing witness to another while feelings are shared honestly heals emotional wounds far faster than trying to go through life alone.

A few weeks later, the truth of that concept was validated for me in an even deeper way.

I had become a volunteer at the Civic Center to continue seeing the plays for which my husband and I previously had tickets for so many years. A certain number of hours are required in exchange for access to the performances. I signed up to help at a film I knew nothing about. I chose it because, having just had a knee surgery I couldn't easily go up and down the stairs of the huge civic center. All I needed to do at the theater for that show was stand at the door and greet people, which worked perfectly. After everyone was seated in the theater, I slipped into a seat toward the back and was riveted by what I saw on the screen.

"Resilience," a 2016 documentary about toxic stress and its affect on physical health, shows a schoolteacher and a pediatrician who wanted to solve the problem of poor school performance and increased doctor visits in their California neighborhood. They had the idea to bring in a compassionate "Ms. Kendra" character to the classrooms of five-, six-, and seven-year-olds to explain what a normal reaction would be toward certain experiences at their age. The children were given a dozen examples such as feeling lonely when going home to an empty house after school, being afraid when hearing a loud gun go off nearby, or feeling confused about what to do when parents got angry and yelled. Then the children were asked to write a letter to explain how their home made them feel. The movie showed these young kids writing letters with their limited word knowledge, folding them up, and putting them in Ms. Kendra's pretend mailbox. She left the room and a few days later the kids received a letter back telling them she totally understood how they felt and that she would most likely feel the same way if she were going through the same experience.

Validating what they felt was all it took to completely reverse behavioral and health problems. Their individual circum-stances didn't change. Guns still went off in the neighborhood, and they still lived in the same home environment. However, when the children knew what they felt was normal and were able to express their feelings and have them compassionately validated, they *felt* normal and developed resilience. The turnaround time was amazing. School performance went up and doctor visits went down by 75% percent in just a few short weeks.

My research and experience had been saying the exact same thing! Resilience is built each time a fear is faced, not ignored, or pushed away. When someone is struggling, the most helpful thing is to be heard. This is why the children in the "Resilience" movie were able to make such dramatic shifts. Unfortunately, the discussion among a panel of community leaders that followed the movie cited money as an issue for not implementing the program in schools. It seemed like a simple solution—especially since not spending the money would be more costly in the long run as it would lead to disease, homelessness, prison time, and possible early death.

And then I realized how often I had done this to myself—decided that my emotions weren't worth the time and energy.

Shortly after the movie, I had the opportunity to validate another grandson when I went to visit him in California. He was five years old at the time and was skateboarding alongside me when he suddenly flopped on the grass. I thought he had tripped on something, but when I turned around and asked him what happened, he tearfully answered, "I miss Grandpa being with you, Grandma."

Whew! It stung. His comment even took the breath out of me, but I knew not to negate what he felt. I gave him a big hug and responded gently, "I get it. Me too, hon. It's so disappointing, isn't it? But we can't control what other people choose."

I was so surprised when he stopped crying immediately. Acknowledgment with kindness was all it took to put his sadness behind him. We made our way home smiling and laughing together.

> *"The human soul doesn't want to be advised or fixed or saved. It simply wants to be witnessed, exactly as it is."*
>
> ~ Palmer Parker ~

Confidence in God and The Dance of Life

As I reflected on my experience with my grandson, I felt so incredibly thankful. How amazing that, even though I had made a choice to volunteer for a movie based on an injured knee, it was the exact perfect film for me to watch in that moment while I was learning to validate my own emotions. Seeing it right before that moment with him was another treasured blessing, as I knew exactly how to respond, even when I was feeling overwhelmed and triggered myself.

I suddenly felt incredibly supported. All I had done was ask for a new listening ear and a gal appeared on my path within minutes. As I began listening to my body, noticing emotions and following what resonated, a film showed up to say, "You're on the right track."

It had all begun when I "just happened" to have a panic attack in the middle of the night. By way of asking for some help and seeking counsel when given the term Narcissistic/Codependent, I "just happened" to discover the latest science, which "just happened" to lead me to the mind-body connection, which "just happened" to get me to the movie "Resilience."

So many "just happening" events made me think things were not "just happening." Life was happening *for me not to me*, completely turning around as I began to notice what was *felt*. I had been so entrained to use the 5% percent, not the 95%, to navigate life that my mind and body were disconnected. And now, listening to my body is what allowed me to use my mind to connect the two. Rather than my mind focused on what was happening "out there" it was focused "on me" and mirroring the values in my heart.

The difference in moving forward in life was like night and day. Instead of making decisions by going back and forth in my head, trying to decide between "this or that," I noticed what felt soft, gentle and expansive versus critical, harsh, and/or constrictive. It was so much easier. I stopped getting stuck in indecision, and this faster and better decision-making brought peace of mind more quickly. The faster the choice, the less stress. Life seemed to go so much smoother, and I was developing confidence in my ability to make good choices on my behalf.

The Indomitable Human Spirit

I always heard phrases such as "Listen to your heart," "Open your heart," and "Follow your heart." These expressions tend to resonate with all of us. For thousands of years, every culture and religion across the planet resonated with a similar belief that the heart is a source of intelligence. They all believe the heart not only encompasses some of the highest values we have as humans, but it associates the highest quality feelings. Its intelligence has been the source of connection, morality, ethical solutions, healings, and guidance.

Physically, the heart is merely a small, ten-ounce muscle that pumps blood through our system. Energetically, it's a data processing center, an electrical organ that sends electrical signals to the brain. The brain's amygdala listens, translates the signals and the thalamus correlates chemicals. The heart pumps these chemicals to every organ via the vagus nerve that runs up and down the spine.

The heart produces enough electrical energy that it creates an electromagnetic field that surrounds the body 360 degrees. Signals from the heart are 55,000 times stronger than knowledge from the head. They extend beyond the skin, out into space, measurable up to about 3 feet outside the body. This electromagnetic field influences everything—more influential to health and well-being than all other factors combined.

The Intuitive Heart

The heart communicates an amazingly wide spectrum of information for mental and physical health, but it has a deeper source of wisdom. Charles Stanley wrote in his book *The Gift of Heaven* that "intuition is knowledge that you and I have without a conscious action on our part. It's a God-given and innate knowledge, a core component that enables one to have an intimate, loving, and overwhelmingly and unimaginably close relationship with God."

We tend to think of intuition as a hunch or gut instinct. But it's more than that. Neuroscientists have discovered that the heart has 40,000 sensory neurons independent of the amygdala that reacts to fear. This intuitive knowing communicates with the brain's pineal gland, a pinecone-shaped organ in the middle of the brain with rods and cones that act like antennae. Our thoughts determine information received. When the pineal gland is open, not only are we curious about what's happening but, we're more able to notice internal cues and surrounding cues. Whereas the mind drifts, loses focus, and gets disoriented, this intuition is a steady presence, resilient and relentless. When conditioned to ignore emotions, we tend to ignore our innate knowing and react to events, figure things out logically and fail to notice all the intuitive hits, the people, resources, and synchronicities right in front of us. Intuition helps us discern what's not quite right and gives us the power to do the "right thing" when facts are confusing, and things get really tough.

In other words, the *heart brain* is talking to the *head brain*. Our heart is talking to us. The question is "are we listening?"

Confidence in Myself

Everyone in the group had been practicing being "present" for a while and was so vulnerable, but denying emotions was so natural for me that it took a while to even tell the difference between facts versus emotions. The two go hand-in-hand like a hand in a glove, and the difference between the two is often so subtle. In fact, I called one of the women after the group one day to apologize if I hurt her feelings. We were having similar experiences but handling them in different ways. I thought I may have come across as judgmental and not empathic. Her response was another eye-opener: "What you feel and how you handle things has nothing to do with me. Feel free to speak to what you are present to. If it triggers something within me, it's my issue."

As I kept listening and felt increasingly safe to share, I was more able to tell the difference between the two languages—head (facts) versus body (emotions). The beauty of being able to speak in a non-judgmental atmosphere is that we can be vulnerable with our most personal, nitty-gritty, intimate fears. The fear of being judged creates stress and makes it easier to stay in our protective shell to avoid internal pressure.

Self-Confidence and Resilience

Confidence is the ability to be ourselves without having to put on a show or an act to be something other than who we are. It's the ability to tell the truth without embellishing, regardless of how others accept the truth. As we accept ourselves and show up honestly and authentically just as we are—regardless of the consequences or how others accept us—it creates a deep sense that we can handle the emotional outcome of life no matter what challenge comes our way. Self-confidence is knowing that we're connected to a Presence within that knows everything but not affected by anything.

Resilience isn't enhanced by ego—at all. Ego takes the quick fix, the easy route and chooses image and distractions to avoid being vulnerable. It takes other people's energy and uses other ways to self-soothe and avoid the truth.

The first step to feeling self-confident is noticing what's felt and learning how to ride the waves of emotions. As we become more aware of how we feel and allow the breath (Hebrew word: spirit) to act like a surfboard that carries the wave of emotional energy through us, the conscious (the 5%) can be bypassed. Even though we naturally fear that emotions will take over our entire life and create delays and inconveniences, the true time it takes an emotion to pass is the equivalent to recovering from a stubbed toe or hitting your elbow—about ninety seconds.

The paradox of life is that we are at our greatest when we are vulnerable, and we will choose to be vulnerable if we think we can handle one or more of the seven common emotions. We don't need to dig up the past to find what caused fear. It can be helpful, but it's more important to be aware of fear as it pops up throughout the day. When able to say, "Hey, I can handle this." the brain is an obedient servant and does whatever we command it to do. Just as a muscle develops strength, flexibility and balance when pushing against resistance, emotional strength, flexibility and balance is developed when pushing against fear. As heavy emotions release through the cardio-vascular system, self-worth increases. With more self-worth, we're more willing to make compassionate, common-sense choices. We don't need to know the future. We just need to know that we can handle the future.

The most common emotions that pull us back are the following eight:

Sadness

Fear

Shame

Anger

Helplessness

Embarrassment

Disappointment

Frustration

Replacing Fear with Truth

The art and science of life is knowing what we want and then believing we can get there. We can sympathize, blame, shop until we drop, drink a fourth glass of wine, medicate, and numb all we want. But until we have a relationship with our body and allow emotions to be our messengers, our ability to think beyond current reality and experience the uncommon is stifled. When our inner narrative shifts, our outer world shifts.

It made sense to my logical mind that, in order to get anywhere, I needed to have an open heart and mind. I had to feel everything to rise above the survival apps that had twisted my DNA. Rather than resist emotions, I took a deep breath and welcomed them all—the knots in my stomach and every single negative thought that caused anger, anxiety, and overwhelm—and used the breath to act as the surfboard to ride the wave.

I also knew I wanted to do something with the science I was discovering and using, but what? I had no idea. All I knew, at this point, was to continue paying attention to what felt like *fight-or-flight* versus *rest-and-digest*, *open* versus *closed*, *expansive* versus *constrictive*; and then to focus on replacing survival apps that got downloaded into my nervous system during childhood, I changed the FEAR acronym "False Entries Assumed Right" to "Feel Everything And Rise."

FEAR—Feel Everything And Rise

1. I am unworthy.

    The truth is: I AM worthy. To think any human is unworthy is denigrating to God's art.

2. I am to believe God is with me—but I can't trust me or my emotions.

The truth is: Light is within me, breathing me, flowing through me, in me, as me. To know what I'm subconsciously thinking, I *have* to trust what I'm consciously feeling.

3. I am broken—undeserving of love.

    The truth is: I AM deserving of love and all things that I love.

4. I am to believe Jesus is God's one and only son.

    The truth is: I AM also a "one and only" unique expression of love.

5. I am small; God is big.

    The truth is: I AM human—the two are One. The *hu* is my spirit; the *man* is my body.

6. I am to consider emotions irrelevant.

    The truth is: I AM an emotional body—which holds 95% of my thoughts.

7. I am unable; God is in control.

    The truth is: I AM interacting with Life with my own free will.

8. I am incapable of making good choices.

    The truth is: I AM capable of handling the outcome of every choice.

9. I am to deny self and serve others first.

    The truth is: I AM to deny childhood perceptions and protect my heart first.

10. I am to obey the rules, think, say, and do whatever authorities say.

    The truth is: I AM to speak the truth in love—no matter what authorities rule.

11. I am meant to suffer through this life to enjoy the next one.

The truth is: I AM to rise above suffering and enjoy this life while living.

12. I am to forgive and "let go" of abusive actions over and over.

The truth is: I AM to "let go" of abusing myself over and over.

As I told fear to take a flying leap, CRAP tied together with emotional knots began to unravel. Love began to rise. My chest felt lighter as more light entered cells. I could see things more clearly as cell shapes became more crystalline. Colors seemed brighter. Coffee smelled better. Birds seemed to chirp more. I knew what fight-or-flight hormones felt like versus rest-and-digest; and with the guessing game over, I understood them but didn't understand them. I went with what resonated but didn't know where I was going. As I trusted emotions and became a better listener, I could listen better to the emotions of others and trust whether their actions came from love or fear. Without feeling compelled to change them, or me, I could avoid arguments when thoughts, facts and opinions didn't match my own. I could spot manipulative games and avoid being pulled into defense mode. I could stay calm in the midst of threats and cautious with demands that made no sense. Rather than procrastinate, I followed my intuition and took baby steps more quickly. Baby steps turned into bigger steps; bigger steps turned into golden opportunities; golden opportunities turned into a world filled with beauty, magic and wonder.

I was coming home to the heart of who I AM. My mind was being reprogrammed to have a healthy independence as it synced with heart qualities. As I allowed the heart to lead the way and the mind to listen, it was as if the two were walking together, hand-in-hand, side-by-side. Self-compassion became a self-fulfilling prophecy.

It all began by noticing the energy fueling my cells. All of them depended on which thoughts I chose.

"The glory of God is a human person fully alive."
~ Iranaeus ~

Trusting My Wings and Flying On My Own

Acknowledging what was *felt* was changing my life—but the process of applying difficult lessons is not always an easy decision. Something came up that got my heart pounding. It tested my resolve, and I almost lost confidence in myself.

My birthday was coming up—the first one without a spouse to help me celebrate. As I considered how lonely it would feel to celebrate alone, I sat down to brainstorm ideas that sounded fun. One idea was to go visit my daughter in D.C. I called her to see if it would be okay and if she'd like to spend a day at the spa. She was excited about the idea, so I bought my plane ticket.

Six weeks later, as I was preparing for the trip, my daughter called and said her job would be sending her out on an assignment and she wouldn't be able to keep our plans. As a news producer, she covered many out-of-town stories. I understood completely but was so disappointed.

Now what? I wondered as I already had the plane ticket. I looked online for something else I could do in D.C. and noticed a free conference being held at a nearby hotel the entire three-day weekend. It sounded interesting, and I decided to sign up.

The conference room was huge, filled with hundreds of upbeat and excited people. The sessions shared the art and science of how people can achieve their dreams.

Seriously? I almost couldn't believe I was listening to more evidence presented to me, showing up so serendipitously, as these lessons confirmed everything I had been studying on my own the past several years. Because of the depth of the topics and the transformational stories, I knew this was my next step in being able to share my own research and transformation with others.

Wow! I really want to do this!

Becoming certified as a Life Coach was so appealing; but when I saw the cost, I realized it was far too expensive.

My budget was cut in half with the divorce, and I'm still unsure of my finances.

As I sat there on the last evening, thinking about all the other events that had transpired when I followed my intuition, I decided to take a leap of faith and signed up in the last fifteen minutes.

My heart was pounding as I returned to my daughter's home. I laid in bed that night with my stomach churning as I listened to the voice of fear trying to talk me out of it: *"What were you thinking? Are you crazy? This is so irresponsible—you can't afford it!"* Fear gripped me as tightly as if an elephant were on my chest. I knew stress hormones were rushing through my body and I wanted them to leave quickly, so I made the decision to call and cancel the next morning. Apparently, the leaders know the pull of the mind that wants to stay safe and made the program non-refundable.

I came home too embarrassed to mention to anyone what I had so foolishly done. The only thing I could do was delve into the material to make the best of it and not waste my investment.

Over the course of the next several months, I put my heart and soul into the coaching course, listened diligently to the CDs, studied the lessons, and then flew out to California to be certified.

Within a week of my return home, there was a check in the mail from the government for double the cost of the program.

What the heck is this? I wondered as I called the number on the letter, thinking the check didn't belong to me and had been issued in error. After making multiple phone calls and being on hold for hours, I finally talked to someone who could give me an answer. It turned out that it was mine after all. It took several more days to realize the money might be linked to my leap of faith.

Seriously? Is this how God works? Is this the result of trusting my intuition?!?

I could hardly contain my excitement. I always had faith and knew God worked in mysterious ways ... but not like this.

Step by step, I was being led down a path to where there was no doubt in my mind that if I continued to trust my heart—not try to understand with just intellect—I'd have to take a crazy leap of faith at times but would somehow land on a featherbed.

Life was becoming more fun and exciting with less doubt and dread about an unknown future. This new way to navigate life made me feel like a kid on Christmas morning—eager to wake and see what surprise would show up next.

What do I want to do with this Life Coaching program? Hmmm...

CHAPTER FIVE
Flying Free
Beautiful Dreamer

"You don't have to be great to start but
you have to start to be great."

~ Zig Ziglar ~

Setting Goals and Expecting Our Highest Good

I knew the life-coaching program would be helpful for so many. It was based on both scientific and spiritual principles and reinforced everything I had learned my entire life. It was upbeat and fun and resonated with my own way of learning, and I knew it would resonate with others. But I didn't know how to let people know what I had to offer.

I woke up one morning thinking a book would be a good idea, but I had never written a book. I have two science degrees, spent hours in the lab using my mind to analyze blood cells and chemical reactions to diagnose diseases. I didn't know how or where to start to write a book. Following the burning desire to share this life-giving knowledge with others, I began to put thoughts on paper and made a commitment to write something every day. I probably went through a hundred drafts in the following year or so until I finally got the nerve to ask someone to read it. The feedback I received was that my writing was too scientific. Interest in facts was lost after the first chapter.

The feedback was disappointing and frustrating but thinking practice makes perfect, I went back to rewrite.

Several months later, I asked someone else to read a new draft. Same response. Too many facts. *Dang*! After four more attempts and getting the same feedback, I was ready to call it quits. Each time, I was told to tell my story and not give so many facts.

The thought of sharing my story was daunting. I didn't want my family embarrassed, and I didn't think anyone would want to hear yet another story of betrayal when so many had been on the news lately. As it turns out, that is not true at all. People trust vulnerable people. Our brain wants to make sense of what doesn't make sense, and people want to hear stories to know what changes they need to make in order to avoid ever becoming a victim again. It made sense. Everyone has a story. Not everyone has a science degree. (Even my counselor looked at me like a deer in headlights when I tried to explain the inner workings of the cell)

After writing several more drafts, and not liking what I wrote, I finally decided this idea wasn't a good one. It was time to find another.

Now what? I kept thinking about possibilities. None of them seemed quite right.

Meanwhile, I continued doing things that brought joy in the daily routine of life and practiced noticing emotions and releasing unwarranted fear. Some of my friends thought I might be bored and lonely at home and offered me a job; but I was having fun with all the research and finding excitement in asking for things I would love and seeing how they'd magically show up.

A few days later, I got a phone call from my neighbor who asked if I would help her friend going through a similar experience.

"Sure, have her give me a call," I offered.

I found myself feeling excited, not for her situation but for an opportunity to help her get past it. I wanted to test what had worked for me with someone else. It was a perfect one-on-one opportunity.

A few days later, I welcomed her into my home. We sat on the back patio, and I began the conversation by asking her to share her story. With shame and anger, she began to relay the details of the past year. Her story was so similar to mine. Even though he had the affair, blame was shifted onto her, and she was taking on the guilt, feeling so bad for messing up what was once a good thing. She was trying so hard to fix things and I assured her she was not responsible for his affair, that he had free will just like her. I gave her a few more tips that worked for me and she left an hour later with more courage, not outrage, saying, "Ahhhh. I can breathe. Thank you so much."

I hadn't done much ... but it felt good to help.

Simply being a witness to another's pain IS powerful!

A few days later, I ran into someone at the bookstore who was in the same Divorce Care class I had attended.

"Hey, what's up?" I asked when she spotted me.

She said her divorce was still dragging on and that she was still fighting for her fair share of assets.

"Oh my gosh. I am so sorry. It's been almost two years!" I said, my heart breaking for her.

She nodded, looking completely drained, her face distraught. She told me that her husband would promise one thing and do another. Unless they could agree on the terms, the case was headed to trial, which would be really costly. She was so ready to "give in," settle, and let him have what he wanted before she lost everything. She also noted how well-rested I looked—said she wished she had been able to end things and move on with her life as quickly as I had. "I would love to just get one good night's sleep."

I could certainly empathize. I remembered those days too when desperately wanting relief. When all the effort I had placed on serving my husband backfired, my head was spinning. Even though I was told the facts of what was happening, I was emotionally overwhelmed. I had been so confused and was so worn out fighting for my rights and trying one more thing.

I offered what I learned about not "giving in" to his facts that triggered her emotions.

"When he can't control your emotions, it'll unnerve him, and you'll be able to think more clearly; then you can more easily negotiate assets by having him think he won."

It is such a stupid game Narcissists play, but this approach tends to end things more quickly. She was more than willing to try. I also offered the supplements I took to support my body when under so much stress. She wrote them down and thanked me for so much advice. Again, I hadn't done much—just listened and offered up two suggestions that had worked for me.

I suddenly realized all the knowledge I had learned was similar to the caterpillar eating leaf after leaf. I had been on a spiritual journey my entire life where everything I did to self-improve was to follow the facts of the day. To stay in shape physically, I learned all I could about nutrition and exercise—which seemed to morph often. To stay in shape spiritually, I attended church faithfully and studied the Bible—translations morphed too. When I tried my best following all the rules and life fell apart anyway, my logic knew I needed to find a new way of doing things. With research and support, I was led down a path to learn the truth of what was happening. As I dug deeper, what I uncovered was that most of what I had been taught was backwards. It allowed others to run my life.

The irony is that everything I had consumed over the course of my life was now being used to do what I had always wanted to do— love others well. I chose the medical field to understand how cells physically work, and I just spent the past several years to understand how they energetically work. Rather than look at visible results as a technologist, I know the invisible root cause of disease and have better ways to help.

It dawned on me that hurting people could care less about how they got to where they are, what hormones run through the bloodstream, how the brain works, or how stress closes cells. I was the one fascinated with the facts. Most want the Readers Digest version—how to reverse results to *feel* better. And I knew the answer: honor the Truth of who we are. Emotions are our truth-teller. Loving well begins with a to-BE list, not a to-do list.

Life isn't about avoiding the twists and turns—getting things right or wrong. It's about who we're becoming along the way.

Research tells us that when we live a life that is guided by an awareness of what matters most to us—otherwise known as our *core values*—we exhibit lower stress, more confident decision-making and problem-solving skills, better attention to health, and more willpower to persist at difficult tasks. We have the ability to act more assertively, communicate with more compassion, and make wiser career and work choices; we have a stronger sense of confidence and enhanced relationship intimacy. The power that's breathing us, moving within us and is us is always seeking to express itself through us. "I AM" is the author, and the sentence is my life. Discovering who we are and are meant to be doesn't come from what we think we can do but from what this Spirit moving within us can do.

We all have core values, whether we're aware of them or not. Once identified, you might shift your daily schedule to include more time for yourself, more time with friends or more time to exercise your creativity. While core values can sometimes shift and change over time—depending on our life circumstances and discoveries—for the most part, they remain stable over the course of our lives. The result: a life lived in harmony with what's most important and life filled with greater purpose. People who don't trust emotions don't trust their own moral compass and lose touch with what really matters. They live lives on autopilot, passively making decisions in the rush of everyday life without taking the time to reflect on what's most important. They worry about their status, position, or power and tend to protect their turf, and keep emotions, people, dreams—and intuition—at bay.

Values are the underlying principles that we hold as most important. Every action we take, consciously or not, comes from an underlying value—one we likely learned and embodied through a combination of things like family experience, culture, role models, and life experience. Values act as a barometer for how we grow, evolve, and change over time. We can use them as a filter for making decisions about everything.

Emotions are what make us human. We can't be thinking the same old thoughts and hold fast to values when emotions have been the black sheep in our culture. New neurons are needed to welcome them. We all know that challenges are part of life; but to "come as we really are" had us all think there must be something wrong with us. We all falsely thought that if we just confess our sins, pray more, and submit to what others say is the will of God for us that life would go well for us later. But what about this life? Most would rather feel negative emotions than nothing at all. Thoughts go a hundred miles an hour and it makes us feel like something is happening. But we stay stuck and paralyzed in anxious places where poison flows in us and from us. An inner disturbance creates an outer disturbance. Keeping secrets keeps us isolated. Days run through our fingers like fine sand and we can't stop it. The whole thing is going so fast. And often we have to be on the edge of losing our mind before we begin to value it and think about what really matters.

The beauty of living in integrity is that we don't have to put a face on things. Emotions reveal who we're becoming and who we're unbecoming. Trust awakens our heart and mind; appreciation allows us to be satisfied with what is and look forward to more. Emotions can breathe life into our deflated souls and lift the curtain of fear hiding our trembling hearts. They give us the courage to stand our ground, take honorable risks and live the life our heart wants. They give us the will to say *yes* to life and *no* to the lies that keep us hidden.

The unlived life is the greatest sin. Noticing chemicals that run through the bloodstream allows us to *feel* what gives life. It's through the body that we'll *know.* If we don't notice how we feel, how can we make the decisions that are best for us? As the mind decrees the body is safe, chemicals shift. Ultimate self-love is finding appreciation in each moment. Appreciation is a powerful energy associated with abundance. Research proves that the reciprocal relationship between visible cells and invisible emotions is that we can think better when our body is at rest—and our body is at rest as we think better thoughts.

My knowledge is still being used to please people, not by fixing their problems, but by empowering them to fix them. As the mind and body become one, not only do we sort out, honor and live our values, but cells thrive and our intuitive voice comes in loud and clear. The more willing we are to trust our inner GPS, the more success we experience along the way.

As I took a stand for personal responsibility, the small box I was in opened to see a world of possibilities that was never there before. I had to be in the opposite end of the spectrum— compassionate toward myself to perceive a compassionate world out there. "Letting go" fear allowed me to spot and stop those who enjoy creating fear, and allow them to go find their own way home to the heart of who they are.

I gained much more than head knowledge. I gained freedom.

Childhood programming isn't our fault, but it is our "response-ability" to stop defaulting to survival apps that aren't necessary anymore. Everything happens for a reason, and it was really hard to admit that most of the time the reason was me. Like Dorothy, on her yellow brick road, I was put in a box during childhood, worked in a box as an adult, ate lunch from a box, and am thankful I didn't die in a box and call it a life. Wisdom comes from being in the dark. We can't get it any other way. The dark night of the soul is like a Divine tap on the shoulder saying "Hey, I'm here too!" I still have stressful moments and get caught off-guard at times. The only difference now is that I recognize fear for what it is and can move past it more quickly. As Glinda, the good witch, said at the end of Dorothy's journey: "You always had the power, my dear. You just had to learn it for yourself."

Meanwhile, I was getting more phone calls from other women who knew someone who knew me, confirming the fact that we really aren't separated from each other. Everyone is connected in this quantum field of Light. It reminded me of the six degrees of separation theory I heard years ago—the idea that we're not separated from each other by more than six people. I was beginning to think the number should go down to three.

One woman called for help to survive an emotionally abusive marriage. She had heard I recovered from one and wondered how in the world I was able to do so without losing my sanity. After our conversation, she told me I was the first person who "got it" —that she had no one who understood the crazy making she was going through. In addition, she was so busy holding down a job, trying to manage the home, and be there for her kids that she had no counseling available and no time to do any research. She had no clue about the classic signs of manipulation or the typical, predictable cycle of a Narcissist and was trying so hard to do the *right* thing. One hour on the phone gave her so much relief that she asked if she could call me back the next day.

"Of course," I said. "Anytime."

Another woman called me during mediation for support. She was taking a break from the intensity in the room. She said he was refusing to sign papers, stonewalling so she would give up her fair share of the assets. I was able to encourage her to detach emotionally and stick to her fair share. She called me later that night to tell me he had finally signed a fair deal, thank me profusely, and say she wished we lived closer so we could celebrate—even though we had never met in person.

Another woman remarried shortly after her last divorce and was on her second divorce within months. Both relationships started out great but, within a year, turned possessive, demeaning, and controlling. She had little confidence in knowing who and who not to trust, and the idea of trusting anyone anymore was unnerving. I was able to explain "through her body and blood" *how* to regain trust in her "still, small voice" and avoid unknowingly repeating the same scenario.

Another woman was told she should try harder to meet his needs even though everything he was doing went against her core values. I was able to help her identify what mattered most to her so that she could protect what's important.

Another woman was told that marriage wasn't meant to be happy—to work things out, even though he left the home. Honestly, I had to laugh at that one. How was *she* was supposed to work things out when *he* wasn't even there?

Another woman was told to trust God, humble herself and take care of her husband's needs. She was being guilted for feeling the way she did, didn't know if he did or didn't truly intend to hurt her feelings, and found herself trying to decide what to do. I was able to encourage her with an adamant, "Yes! Trust that God wants your best. Come back to center and stop second-guessing your husband's intentions. With a few more tips, she was less confused.

Another woman was told she needed to be "flexible" in her marriage, even though she was clearly being manipulated. I was able to tell her, "It's true. Being flexible is great. AND you need to first consider if you are becoming "flexible" with the wrong person, or without good reason, or with one of your values that's simply not open to compromise." With just a few facts, she felt less guilty.

My heart went out to these women. They were at their wits' end, trying so hard to *do* the right thing, rather than *be* in their natural state. They sought help from authoritative figures they trusted to give good advice, but the advice was outdated, unscientific, and cruel. I was so thankful I was there to help. I realized how many people needed help, someone who had already been through the transformative process—who understood the load of pain secreted away in favor of rules that made no sense. I wanted to help sort out the confusion, speak the truth in love, and show them another way. The process was tested (by me), and it was safe to share.

How can I make this knowledge available to more? Maybe I could find someone who's good at writing stories to help me finish the book...

One morning, shortly after thinking I should continue writing the book, I received a prayer request from someone in the same life coaching program I had attended. We had met once in a breakout room. After responding to her request, I thought I would do the same and asked if one of the four in the text could help me find support. "Does anyone know a good story writer who could help me with my book?"

A few minutes later, I received a name and number.

Wow! What are the chances?

I quickly texted the number and received a quick reply back.

And she's quick to respond, too?

We set up a time to chat over zoom, and I decided to look at her website in preparation.

Oh my goodness! The butterfly metaphor and all her words. She's not just a good option. It looks like I've found someone who will completely understand my message and has the skills to help me.

I met the message coach on zoom and immediately knew she was the right fit.

She gave me the cost and I had no clue how I was going to afford her; but I have "been there, done that" before and said *yes* quickly before fear rushed in to stop me. Was it scary? Definitely. But I knew this was the great opportunity I had been looking for to pass on valuable information. I took the leap of faith, trusting somehow the money would be handled. How? I couldn't possibly predict.

And here we are.

Living Our Truth & Finding Freedom

On Sunday mornings, I see a beautiful stained-glass window at the back of the church from the choir loft. The entire window is a collection of panes. Each color has become a representation of the places, people, and experiences unique to me.

In this window, the blue panels are the most common. They represent the happy days and how blue skies and easy walks produced serotonin, the "happy hormone." The vibrant reds represent the adrenaline days, like all the times I rushed around to make Christmas and birthday celebrations special. The sunny yellows represent oxytocin days when love for grandkids took them to the beach and treated them to acai bowls after. Black panes represent cortisol days when people made me wonder what the heck was going on, similar to the characters who popped out on Dorothy's yellow brick road with unmet needs of their own.

Those are the days we fight tooth and nail to have things go back to normal. But we can't go back to the way things were. Innocence is gone. Life will never be the same. With raging emotions churning inside, we're like the little chrysalis barely hanging on to the little stick of hope that's left. It's easy to forget that life is happening *for us, not to us.*

I was sitting in the choir loft, waiting for the church service to begin, and noticed the orchestra tuning their own instruments before they tuned with each other.

Wow. This is the symphony of life. Musicians know that they can't play well together until they tune their own instrument.

I've learned so much about how to tune mine and realized how far I had come since that first choir practice years ago.

I had entered the room on edge, guarded, fearful of who would be there. My friend who invited me was the only one in the church who knew what I was going through. I didn't want anyone else to know. I was humiliated. Emotions were raw. Thoughts were running rampant, and I was battling feelings of guilt and shame around letting my husband down, regularly asking myself the question: *Was I that bad of a wife?*

I was shown around the room, told where to put my things, and then followed the director's request to take a seat so rehearsal could begin.

"Welcome everyone," the director started. "Let's pull out the first piece of music and begin with 'Jesus, Friend of the Wounded Heart.'"

I thought my friend arranged it, but she looked at me, stunned. "This is the first song? Seriously?" I asked quietly. In shock and awe, tears welled for both of us. I got a lump in my throat and couldn't sing as I noticed how the title and timing seemed perfect—as if meant just for me.

Perfectly timed events started "just happening" that day. I always had faith and believed all things worked together for good (conceptually), but we can't always see it when we're in it. Who in their right mind would choose days filled with grief? But these orchestrations continued—they've not only been incredible but humbling.

Why do I doubt? I ask when fear creeps up now.

I've gotten to the point where I perk up with anticipation when things turn upside-down. I know what comes next.

I stared at the stained-glass week after week and had another *aha* moment when I noticed white light coming through a crack in one of the panes. Each of the panes represent the ways I danced with that Light, colored events with my own perceptions, each one a part of the whole. Not one can be singled out, but each was recorded for my benefit. Any good interior designer knows that a little black adds depth. Some of my experiences were endearing, and some not worth enduring any more. I truly felt blessed being married to someone smart, funny and goal-oriented. But without trust, it no longer held the same level of passion. For my own good, it was time to fight for my heart and move on. Now a new passion wants to be birthed.

Nature knows no punishment—only consequences. It doesn't apologize for the blacks, the whites, the hundreds of grays; in the end they all work in harmony to create beauty, a colorful world filled with plentiful ideas and multiple choices.

Life itself is transformative—if we allow it to be. As children, we relied on others to help us choose; as adults, we become the authority and unknowingly repeat the same blueprint received as a child. We're not the thoughts from our past or future, nor are we the victim of a capricious God. Being in the dark can either add depth of character or align us more closely to we really are, an individual and creative person with desires and choices. That is really all there ever is: The moment of choice.

As I noticed my moments and chose to rewire my nervous system, life became more of a celebration than an endurance contest. Emotions became a marker not a weapon. Confusion turned to clarity. Shame became my strength. Sadness turned to joy. Grief became a bigger love. One purpose changed for another—one of many as my story continues to unfold.

We can't lose our memories. Nor would we want to. They bring us to where we are now. As I took myself "off the cross" with the fear of others "hanging me," I became more of a masterpiece than a mess. I know my body's not broken; it's working for me on my behalf. Experiences that created doubt no longer control me; I see the benefit of these doubts, recognize them for what they are, and can listen more closely to figure out the right next step. I know there is no reality except the one I'm believing, and I have more ways to embrace the past and create a future with a more mature and fruitful faith. And because I'm ready to love and accept all of me and everything I've been through, I know my truth and the Truth knows me.

When we know better, we want to do better. The window has become a weekly reminder to pause, reflect on the past week, take stock, shake off what didn't work, and build on what did.

What exactly was stressful? Are there any beliefs that need to be let go? What do I want to continue, and what do I want to stop? What is one thing that I can do today to make life better for me, or someone else?

I close my eyes, take a deep breath and let my mind wander. I take mental note of the things that sound lighthearted and fun. Deep down I know that as I AM lighter, others will feel lighter. As I matter more, others will matter more.

Self-love breeds love. Self-empathy breeds empathy. Self-compassion breeds compassion.

CONCLUSION

Time for You to Fly Free

"The intuitive mind is a sacred gift and the rational mind is a faithful servant. We have created a society that honors the servant and has forgotten the gift."

~ Albert Einstein ~

To keep from being bored while manning the butterfly booth, I would grab the attention of anyone who seemed half-way interested and willing to listen to me. The attention of children was pretty easy to grab if I started out with the comment, "Hey, did you know caterpillars can fly?" They would look at me with squinty, skeptical eyes, as if I were playing a joke on them. Doubtful, but curious, they were drawn to the table where we always had all four stages on display. Many had been told about the butterfly transformation in school but had never seen the process in real life.

"A caterpillar can fly, but not as a caterpillar," I would begin.

"This is how it all starts. An egg is laid on the underside of a leaf. Each type of butterfly knows exactly which type plant their babies like to eat."

I would pause to let them find a tiny egg on one of the leaves before pointing to the next stage.

"The caterpillar stage comes after the egg hatches. It's known as the feeding stage because it eats nonstop. It eats, eats, and eats; and when it gets too fat, it sheds its skin, creates a new one, and wants to eat some more. It outgrows and sheds its skin at least five times before it goes to the next stage. Do you guys eat so much that you outgrow your clothes like that?"

The kids would give me a "what the heck" look. Why wouldn't an adult know that? Of course they outgrow their clothes. That's nothing new. What's the point? I let them comment a while before I continued.

"You know what? Caterpillars often get squished at this stage because they eat so much and people, who don't know they're butterflies, think caterpillars are ruining their plants. People knock them off and step on them."

The kids often frowned and became sad, but I'd move on by having them guess the next stage.

"Yep, you're right," I'd reply when "cocoon" was mentioned. (That's what most people think.)

"Cocoon is the pupa stage," I'd say.

"But, did you know that butterflies don't actually form cocoons?"

The kids would look at me totally confused, and I would let them be curious for a moment. I wanted them to be critical thinkers, a pupil in their own stage of learning.

"Butterflies form a chrysalis; moths form cocoons," I simply explained. "Moths fly around at night, aren't nearly as pretty, leave a dirty, sooty mess on things, and people don't really like them very much. Butterflies fly around during the day, have beautiful, crystalline-shaped patterns and colors, and people really like them a lot."

The kids understood. They've seen butterflies and love watching them fly. But now they knew more about them, were excited, and turned around to look at their mom waiting in the aisle and urge her to come over to the booth.

"Hey wait, there's more!" I'd exclaim. They'd stop, but now the moms were interested and came over to listen while the kids eagerly described the cycle as I described it, and then were ready to listen again. "Okay. What's next?" they'd ask.

"If nothing kills the caterpillar, imaginal cells within begin to activate transformation. At first, the caterpillar wiggles and fights it off. Its immune system is compromised at this stage and it's vulnerable to all kinds of things that could kill it— especially as it wiggles to go upside-down and form a protective shell to hide in while it matures into a full adult. Can you imagine what it would feel like when it starts to get dark in there and then when it gets totally dark?"

They'd answer with simple childlike honesty. "I'd be scared! I'd be lonely! I wouldn't do it! I'd be kicking my way out!" The mom and I would smile.

When they tried to touch the chrysalis, I'd stop them. "Don't touch; it's too dangerous. It's hanging on for dear life! If it falls off before maturing, I'd have to glue it back on the stick." And I'd reassure them that the butterfly isn't scared. Even though it's in the dark, and everything about the caterpillar dissolves into goo and gets rearranged, it somehow knows it's going through a natural process.

Some moms were skeptical of me. We were passing out brochures on Master Gardening and they were watching me closely, as if I had another agenda or sales pitch to sell some other product. I didn't, of course. And I didn't take offense. I knew they were trying to protect their kids from taking just anything. I was a protective mama-bear, too, and honored their desire when they didn't have time or want their children to stay. Those who were allowed were mesmerized with the process. Some were present when the butterfly completely broke free. When that happened, I never saw one person leave the booth without being in awe and wonder, thrilled they were there in the right place at the right time to witness that magical moment.

A friend invited me to walk a labyrinth this past year. These are often confused with mazes. Both are similar with twists and turns winding around a path; but they are different. The path of the labyrinth is similar to the spiral of the universe, as seen in the Milky Way, seashells, the core of apples, and even our DNA. You walk the path to the center and then you take the same path out. Unlike a maze, you can't get lost. We might *feel* lost at times, but we're not. We're just twisting and turning, handling life's challenges the best we know how, continually coming back to things we thought we understood.

I heard it said that there are two ways to wake up: great pain or deep love. The idea of losing family, friends, or our life (as is) triggers great pain because we do have great love. Our natural instinct is to fight for it. But when we realize we have no control over what others think, easy answers aren't so easy anymore.

We think of life as going from point A to B. But if we think of life as a spiral, with stages of growth, it is logical to say we go through many spirals throughout our lifetime. Our journey is unique to each of us, but similar in the fact that there's a voice within all of us urging us onward and upward. The Christian message should be we deserve happiness; but too often we settle for less and submit to what others think. Love can set us free—but it often has to make us red-hot mad first. To become all we can become requires creativity and breaking through the fear that stops us. If we are willing to accept the fact that we are emotional beings in a physical skin suit, then every upside-down can be considered a growth spurt to better understand our unique role in this land of the free and the home of the brave.

Knowledge is power. Anytime a player doesn't know his part on the team, the whole team is in trouble. The better the grasp of how the mind-body works the greater potential for the two to work as one team.

Knowing we're connected to the Infinite that knows no space or time and has unlimited ways to find solutions, we can simply spiral back to BE the loving people we are. Any other time than that, we can choose to be quiet to gain understanding. There's always something new, something to learn, something good that can emerge from the dark. Little by little our paradigm will shift, and we'll reclaim our innate ability to heal emotionally and physically.

Life is kind of funny in that the things truly valued, like self-discipline and attitude, have absolutely nothing to do with what's external to us. The hard part, up until now, has been is believing an internal change is what changes external results. Hanging on for dear life, hoping others will change is the definition of insanity. It doesn't mean doing nothing either. Discontent and longing for more is a signal to grow. We can go through the process kicking and screaming or come home to the heart of who we are. It's in the stillness where we see the problem is not the problem. The problem is that we keep thinking and talking about the problem and managing symptoms rather than getting to the root cause.

It's a challenge to look deeply within so that we can look deeply at others. It's tempting to repay evil with evil and insult with insult. To move past our personal reality to create a new personality and still see the injustice requires self-empathy, not self-hatred. Nobody or nothing can use our mind to put our body at ease. It's lifelong journey and it takes a lifetime of practice.

When I look back, I wonder *how in the world I ever believed I was unworthy when God didn't? How did I ever believe heaven was for later when Jesus himself said "heaven is within"? How did I ever believe in punishment when nature knows no punishment, only consequences? And why the heck would I be given emotions if they were meant to be irrelevant?*

It's almost impossible to have emotions and pretend we don't. And it's almost impossible to take moral inventory when thoughts are hidden and emotions are closed off. As Richard Rohr says, "You can't heal what you don't acknowledge… the longer you hide, the sicker you get."

I often wish I had a time machine to go back and start all over. I can't do that, but I can imagine a new future for me, my grandchildren, family, and friends—one where everyone knows they matter … and what matters to them does too. It's how we can gently walk through life, not push our way through—how we can design a life we love instead of defaulting to what is.

By noticing our internal circuitry we won't allow fear to be the fuel or get swept under the rug. We'll go into the parts of ourselves that we don't like very much and take action to let go of toxic thinking, toxic relationships, toxic foods and other toxic habits. As we rise up again and again, thankful for the signal, we can choose to come back to a natural rhythm and activate imaginal cells to seek life-giving, not life-draining, solutions. Answers aren't always easy; but if we don't take emotions seriously, we'll suffer needlessly. We'll stay stuck in our preconceived ideas, view ourselves right and others wrong, and replicate the same old lifestyle. We won't appreciate the gift of struggle and think it's up to us to do someone else's journey and/or suppress concerns at home and in the workplace for fear we'll be outcast or considered a troublemaker. Is it worth it?

I say *no*. What the world needs now are people who can remember the past and release the pain from the past. The impulses to stay in our illusion of comfort, and not address the patterns in front of us, are not worth it. It cost me my health and a forty-four-year relationship. We see what it's costing our government, education, and health systems.

I say let's reverse engineer—use a whole-brain approach to change the meaning of our lives. When we make ourselves the choice instead of the option, what happens is that we realize we do have control.

As we quiet the mind and listen to our hearts, we'll listen to the mind of others and respond with a kind heart.

As we handle our own negative emotions with compassion, we'll be compassionate with those who lack compassion when we cut the energetic cord and wish them well on their own journey.

As we gain resilience, we'll allow others to gain resilience and stop getting in their way.

As we take a stand for personal responsibility, we'll encourage others to take responsibility.

As we handle ordinary emotions, we'll go beyond the ordinary and do extraordinary things.

As we shift from dependence and codependence to a healthy independence, others will shift.

In other words, as we love and accept ourselves, just as we are, we'll love and accept others by being our right and noble selves (even when difficult). We'll have our moments, but moments won't have us. We'll ground ourselves, ask questions, seek answers, and find compassionate, common-sense solutions... and wake up to the fact that we don't have to die to experience heaven on Earth.

Science is here to clarify what man misunderstood: our true nature is Love. Though we trusted our limited understanding, fumbled in the dark, and got turned around, our relentless hearts have been trying to get our attention all along. As we stake our ground on ancient spiritual laws and principles that are scientifically reliable, predictable, and repeatable, love expands. The good news is that it's never too late to claim our birthright. Old cells die and new are born every day.

The Prayer of St. Francis was sung on my wedding day. Even though life took some unexpected turns, and it appeared as if love failed when all my dreams of living together "'til death do us part" fell apart and died, I'm living proof that Love does conquer all. It brought me home to what matters most. The dream to *feel* loved so that I'm able to love others well merely upgraded to another level of understanding.

As I shared in the beginning, a tipping point is that magical moment when an idea, trend, or social behavior crosses a threshold, tips, and spreads like wildfire. As we remember that nothing can separate us from the love of God, we can transform our stories one-by-one. And with an army of angels in the ethereal realm ready to help, Love on the wings of faith and hope will give us the freedom to fly.

You can do whatever is burning in your heart to come forth, but not with the caterpillar image you've held of yourself. No matter what you've been told, you're a child of God—worthy and deserving—free to pursue a life of vitality, loving relation-ships, fun, peace, passion, and purpose. It's not only my hope for you, but it's been God's dream for you all along. Get in touch with that image—it's the real you.

Prayer of St. Francis

Lord, make me an instrument of your peace
Where there is hatred, let me sow love
Where there is injury, pardon
Where there is doubt, faith
Where there is despair, hope
Where there is darkness, Light
And where there is sadness, Joy

Oh, Divine Master,
Grant that I may not so much seek
To be consoled as to console
To be understood as to understand
To be loved as to love.
For it is in giving that we receive
It is in pardoning
That we are pardoned
And it is in dying
That we are born to eternal life.

Ecclesiastes 3:11
He has made everything beautiful in its time.
Also He has put eternity in their hearts,
except that no one can find out the work that God
does from beginning to end.

Resources

Introduction

1. Multiple Contributors. "At a Tipping Point: Education, Learning and Libraries." OCLC Online Computer Library Center, Inc., 2014.

Chapter 1

2. Pediatric Behavioral Health, Cleveland Clinic.

3. Bradshaw, John. *Homecoming*. Random House Publishing, 1990.

4. Frankl, Viktor. *Man's Search for Meaning (4th Edition). Beacon Press, 1992.*

5. Lipton, Bruce. *Biology of Belief.* Hay House Inc., 2016.

6. Van der Kolk, Bessel. *The Body Keeps The Score*. Viking Penguin, 2014.

7. Dispenza, Dr. Joe. *Breaking The Habit of Being Yourself.* Hay House Inc. 2013.

8. Dispenza, Dr. Joe. *Becoming Supernatural*. Hay House, 2017.

9. Ortner, Nick. *The Tapping Solution*. Hay House, Inc. 2013.

10. Lipton, Bruce. *Biology of Belief.* Hay House Inc., 2016.

11. Heart-Math – HeartSpace Clinic. Boulder Creek, CA. 1991.

12. Sweeton, Jennifer. *Trauma Treatment Toolbox*. PESI Publishing, 2019.

13. Dispenza, Dr. Joe. *Becoming Supernatural*. Hay House, 2017.

Chapter 2

14. Arabi, Shahida. *Becoming the Narcissist's Nightmare.* SCW Archer Publishing, 2016.

15. Rosenberg, Dr. Ross. *The Human Magnet Syndrome.* Premier Publishing & Media, 2013.

16. Simon, George. *In Sheep's Clothing.* Parkhurst Brothers, Inc., 1996.

17. Ortner, Nick. *The Tapping Solution.* Hay House, Inc. 2013.

18. Simon, George. *In Sheep's Clothing.* Parkhurst Brothers, Inc., 1996.

19. Durvasula, PhD, Ramani. *Should I Stay or Should I Go?* Post Hill Press, 2015.

20. Brown, Brené. *Daring Greatly.* Penguin Publishing, 2015.

21. Rankin, Lissa. *Mind Over Medicine.* Hay House Inc., 2020.

22. Bancroft, Lundy. *Why Does He Do That?* Penguin Random House, 2003.

23. Kreger, Mason. *Stop Walking on Eggshells.* New Harbinger Publications, 1998.

24. Wright, Simone. *First Intelligence.* New World Library, 2014.

Chapter 3

25. Barsam, Ara Paul. *Reverence for Life: The Words of Albert Schweitzer.* Oxford University Press, 2008.

26. Emoto, Masaru. *The Hidden Messages in Water.* Beyond Words Pub, 2004.

27. Ortner, Nick. *The Tapping Solution.* Hay House, Inc., 2013.

28. Church, PhD, Dawson. *The Genie in Your Genes.* Hay House, Inc., 2007.

29. Simon, George. *In Sheep's Clothing.* Parkhurst Brothers, Inc., 1996.

30. Rankin, Lissa. *Mind Over Medicine.* Hay House Inc., 2020.

31. Durvasula, PhD, Ramani. *Should I Stay or Should I Go?* Post Hill Press, 2015.

32. Bancroft, Lundy. *Why Does He Do That?* Penguin Random House, 2003.

33. Ortner, Nick. *The Tapping Solution.* Hay House, Inc., 2013.

34. Covey, Steven. *The 7 Habits of Highly Effective People.* Fireside, Simon & Schuster, 1989.

35. Ortner, Nick. *The Tapping Solution.* Hay House, Inc., 2013.

36. Silvious, Jan. *Fool-Proofing Your Life.* Waterbrook Press, 1998.

37. Durvasula, PhD, Ramani. *Should I Stay or Should I Go?* Post Hill Press, 2015.

38. Bancroft, Lundy. *Why Does He Do That?* Penguin Random House, 2003.

39. Stout, PhD, Martha. *The Sociopath Next Door.* Harmony/Rodale. 2006.

40. Childre, Martin, and Beech. *The HeartMath Solution.* HeartMath Institute, 1999.

41. Townsend, Dr. John. *Beyond Boundaries.* Zondervan, 2011.

42. Thomas, Katherine Woodward. *Conscious Uncoupling.* Harmony, 2016.

Chapter 4

43. Stanley, Charles. *The Gift of Heaven.* Nelson Thomas, Inc., 2017.

44. Haugt, Kenneth. *Journeying though Grief.* Stephen Ministries, 2021.

45. Palmer, Parker J. *Let Your Life Speak.* Jossey-Bass, 2009.

46. Childre, Martin, and Beech. *The HeartMath Solution.* HeartMath Institute, 1999.

47. Ortner, Nick. *The Tapping Solution.* Hay House, Inc., 2013.

Chapter 5

48. Bradberry, Travis. *Emotional Intelligence 2.0.* Talent Smart, 2009.

49. Cloud, Dr. Henry. *How People Grow.* Zondervan, 2001.

50. Cloud, Dr. Henry. *How People Grow.* Zondervan, 2001.

51. Kabat-Zinn, Jon. *Full Catastrophe Living.* Random House, 2013.

Conclusion

52. Multiple Contributors. "At a Tipping Point: Education, Learning and Libraries." OCLC Online Computer Library Center, Inc., 2014.

More Resources

Al-Anon *Courage to Change – One Day at a Time,* Al-Anon Family Group.

Beattie, Melody. *Codependent No More.* Hazelden Publishing. 1986.

Blanchard, Ken. *The One-Minute Manager.* William Morrow & Co, 1982.

Boyd, Brady. *Addicted to Busy.* David Cook, 2014.

Chalmers, Dr. Jennifer Harley. *His Needs Her Needs.* Revell, 2013.

Fay, Jim. & Funk, David. *Teaching with Love and Logic.* Love & Logic Press, 2016.

Fleming, SJ, David. *What Is Ignatian Spirituality?* Loyola Press, 2008.

Harley, William. *Surviving an Affair.* Revell Publishing, 2013.

Johnson, Stephen. *Humanizing the Narcissistic Style.* Penguin Books Canada, 1987.

Nouwen, Henry. *The Inner Voice of Love.* Doubleday, 1996.

Personality Disorders, Diagnostic and Statistical Manual of Mental Disorders (DSM-5)NIH, 2013.

Romano, Lisa A. *Quantum Tools to Help you Heal Your Life.* Outskirts Press, 2014.

Van der Kolk, Bessel. *The Body Keeps The Score.* Viking Penguin, 2014.

About Kathleen Joan

As a certified DreamBuilder Life Coach, Kathleen helps people design a life they love rather than default to life as is. After thirty-seven years of moving across the country to support her husband's careers, and raising her family in Christian but diverse cultures, she found herself living close to her childhood home so that her husband could pursue a third career. After a few years back home, life turned upside-down. Her forty-decade-plus marriage ended and everything she believed to be true fell away. When she learned she had been living in a narcissistic-codependent relationship, she ventured into science to find the root cause. What she discovered was how easy it is for the mind to be manipulated and how hard it is to change. Learning proven strategies from some of the most heart-centered educators, Kathleen stepped onto the path of transforming her own mind and her life.

Experiencing deeper and deeper levels of freedom, she was inspired to pay forward all she had learned and help others who have found themselves trapped in the narcissist-codependent dynamic so prevalent in our culture. Using the butterfly metamorphosis as a metaphor, her purpose is to bridge new science with ancient spiritual laws and principles. By rearranging biology, unlocking DNA, and clarifying Truth, they come "home" to their true nature—love. Love makes it easy to stand in integrity when values are challenged, be in control when others are out of control, and eventually have and pursue dreams again.

Kathleen is a mom to three and a grandmother to ten. She holds two Bachelor degrees, one in Biology, the other in Medical Technology. She's a trained Stephen Minister, a Master Gardener, has been a mentor to all age groups, and practices daily the art of loving others as she loves herself. She loves to travel, be in nature, volunteer in the community, and gather friends on her back patio for fun conversations and yummy food. Her favorite achievements are savored when her ten grandchildren reach over just to hug and whisper in her ear how much they love her.

Invitation

This book was written to bring more awareness to the narcissistic/ codependent pandemic wreaking havoc in our culture. I wanted to empower with new facts and my new approach to life.

You may have a deeper understanding of what narcissism looks like, but do you know how to stop controlling others and start caring for yourself?

Implementing change, as you saw in my story, is quite a task. You can be in counseling for decades and still be triggered by pain from someone you cared for deeply and who treated you horribly. Grief isn't easy to dismiss and habits are hard to break, especially when they've been part of you forever and "feel" normal.

No time to figure it all out?

Consider DreamBuilding, a program designed to explore your gifts and talents and use the scientific and spiritual laws and principles that govern our Universe to go beyond your past. It has helped tens of thousands transform their lives and achieve extraordinary results no matter what age, condition, or circumstance they find themselves.

Join me to begin to dream new dreams, improve relationships, achieve better health, and/or increase your motivation.

www.FromGooToGratitude.com

"He who is in you is greater than he who is in the world."
~ 1 John 4:4 ~

Made in the USA
Monee, IL
19 May 2023

34080109R00077